Zaner-Bloser
Handwriting
With a simplified alphabet

Author

Clinton S. Hackney

Contributing Authors

Pamela J. Farris
Janice T. Jones
Linda Leonard Lamme

D1608638

Zaner-Bloser, Inc., P.O. Box 16764, Columbus, Ohio 43216-6764   1-800-421-3018

Copyright © 1999 Zaner-Bloser, Inc.   ISBN 0-88085-959-8

Developed by Kirchoff/Wohlberg, Inc., in cooperation teith Zaner-Bloser Publishers

Printed in the United States of America

0I 02 WC 5

You already know handwriting is important.
Now take a look at...

NEW SIMPLIFIED

Zaner-Bloser Handwriting

Easier to read! Easier to write! Easier to teach!

Zaner-Bloser's new program is easy to teach.

I see Zaner-Bloser's alphabet in the books I read.

I like Zaner-Bloser because it's so easy to write.

You already know handwriting is important, but did you know...

Did You Know...

Annually, the U.S. Postal Service receives 38 million illegibly addressed letters, costing American taxpayers $4 million each year.

–American Demographics, Dec. 1992

Did You Know...

Hundreds of thousands of tax returns are delayed every year because figures, notes, and signatures are illegible.

–Better Handwriting in 30 Days, 1989

Did You Know...

Poor handwriting costs American business $200 million annually.

–American Demographics, Dec. 1992

Zaner-Bloser's CONTINUOUS-STROKE manuscript alphabet

Aa Bb Cc Dd Ee Ff Gg
Oo Pp Qq Rr Ss Tt

Easier to Read

Our vertical manuscript alphabet is like the alphabet kids see every day inside and outside of the classroom. They see it in their school books, in important environmental print like road signs, and in books and cartoons they read for fun.

"[Slanted] manuscript is not only harder to learn than traditional [vertical] print, but it creates substantially more letter recognition errors and causes more letter confusion than does the traditional style."

> –Debby Kuhl and Peter Dewitz in a paper presented at the 1994 meeting of the American Educational Research Association

Please, my friends, a moment of silence, as the flying Zucchinis attempt a twisting triple somersault.

CALIFORNIA LIN 216

STOP

Vertical manuscript is the alphabet we see every day.

CIRCUS by Lois Ehlert ©1992 by Lois Ehlert

Hh Ii Jj Kk Ll Mm Nn
Uu Vv Ww Xx Yy Zz

Easier to Write

Our vertical manuscript alphabet is written with continuous strokes—fewer pencil lifts—so there's a greater sense of flow in writing. And kids can write every letter once they learn four simple strokes that even kindergartners can manage.

Four simple strokes: circle, horizontal line, vertical line, slanted line

"The writing hand has to change direction more often when writing the [slanted] alphabet, do more retracing of lines, and make more strokes that occur later in children's development."

–Steve Graham in *Focus on Exceptional Children,* 1992

Many kids can already write their names when they start school (vertical manuscript).

Kirk

Why should they have to relearn them in another form (slanted manuscript)? With Zaner-Bloser, they don't have to.

Kirk

Easier to Teach

Our vertical manuscript alphabet is easy to teach because there's no reteaching involved. Children are already familiar with our letterforms—they've seen them in their environment and they've learned them at home.

"Before starting school, many children learn how to write traditional [vertical] manuscript letters from their parents or preschool teachers. Learning a special alphabet such as [slanted] means that these children will have to relearn many of the letters they can already write."

–Steve Graham in *Focus on Exceptional Children,* 1992

Zaner-Bloser's NEW SIMPLIFIED cursive alphabet

Aa Bb Cc Dd Ee Ff Gg

Nn Oo Pp Qq Rr Ss

Simplified letterforms...
Easier to read and write

old letterform

Letterforms are simplified so they're easier to write and easier to identify in writing. The new simplified **Q** now looks like a **Q** instead of a number 2.

old letterform

Our simplified letterforms use the headline, midline, and baseline as a guide for where letters start and stop. The new simplified **d** touches the headline instead of stopping halfway.

old letterform

No more "cane stems"! Our new simplified letterforms begin with a small curve instead of fancy loops that can be difficult for students to write.

Hh Ii Jj Kk Ll Mm
Tt Uu Vv Ww Xx Yy Zz

Simplified letterforms...
Easier to teach

When handwriting is easy for students to write, instruction time is cut way back! That's the teaching advantage with Zaner-Bloser Handwriting. Our cursive letterforms are simplified so instead of spending a lot of time teaching fancy loops that give kids trouble, teachers give instruction for simple, basic handwriting that students can use for the rest of their lives.

These simple letters are so much easier to teach!

And remember, with Zaner-Bloser Handwriting, students learn to write manuscript with continuous strokes. That means that when it's time for those students to begin writing cursive, the transition comes naturally because they already know the flow of continuous strokes.

The Student Edition...set up for student success

Letter models show stroke direction and sequence.

Letters are grouped and taught by the strokes used to form them.

Students first practice letters, then joinings, and finally complete words.

Helpful hints assist students in avoiding common handwriting problems.

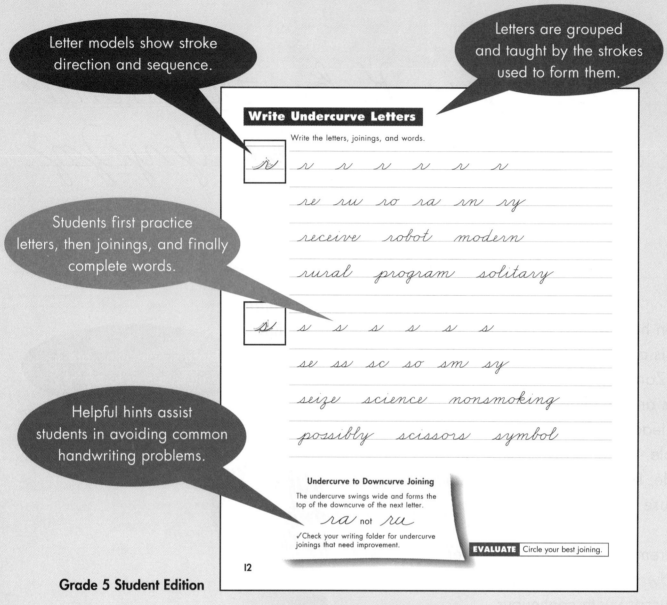

Write Undercurve Letters

Write the letters, joinings, and words.

r r r r r r

re ru ro ra rn ry

receive robot modern

rural program solitary

s s s s s s

se ss sc so sm sy

seize science nonsmoking

possibly scissors symbol

Undercurve to Downcurve Joining

The undercurve swings wide and forms the top of the downcurve of the next letter.

ra not *ru*

✓Check your writing folder for undercurve joinings that need improvement.

EVALUATE Circle your best joining.

12

Grade 5 Student Edition

Prewriting • Drafting • Revising • Editing • Publishing

Students are taught the relationship between handwriting and the writing process through activities like this one. Here, students use each step of the writing process to write about a journey.

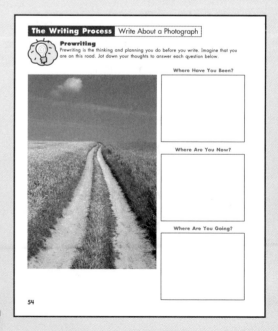

The Writing Process Write About a Photograph

Prewriting
Prewriting is the thinking and planning you do before you write. Imagine that you are on this road. Jot down your thoughts to answer each question below.

Where Have You Been?

Where Are You Now?

Where Are You Going?

54

Write Lead Sentences

A lead sentence is the first sentence of a story. It may tell *who*, *what*, *when*, and *where*. Sometimes it tells *why*.

James Wilson Marshall discovered gold
who — what

at Sutter's Mill this morning
where — when

Use the facts to write lead sentences.

Who: *Mrs. O'Leary's cow*   Where: *in the O'Leary barn*
What: *kicked over a lantern*   When: *last night*

Who: *Abolitionist Sojourner Truth*
What: *spoke*   When: *yesterday*
Where: *at Seneca Falls*   Why: *to get voting rights*

On Your Own Write a lead sentence about either a school event or a historical event. Try to include the five W's: *who*, *what*, *when*, *where*, and *why*.

EVALUATE Is there space for ○ between letters?   Yes   No

69

Grade 5 Student Edition

Drafting
Drafting means putting your ideas into sentences for the first time. Use your answers to the prewriting questions as you draft an entry in your travel diary about your journey. Remember to write legibly.

COLLISION ALERT Make sure your tall letters do not bump into the descenders above them.

EVALUATE Did you avoid collisions?   Yes   No
Is your writing legible?   Yes   No

55

Revising and Editing

When you revise your writing, you make sure it says just what you mean. When you edit, you find and correct errors in spelling, capitalization, punctuation, and handwriting. Use the checklist below as you revise and edit your draft. You may ask a friend to read your draft and help you answer the questions.

Does your writing include all the information readers will want to know?	Yes	No
Does your writing include descriptive details?	Yes	No
Are all words spelled correctly?	Yes	No
Have you used uppercase letters and punctuation correctly?	Yes	No
Do your letters have good shape?	Yes	No
Do your letters rest on the baseline?	Yes	No
Are short letters half the height of tall letters?	Yes	No
Does your writing have uniform slant?	Yes	No
Are there good spaces between letters, words, and sentences?	Yes	No
Is your writing easy to read?	Yes	No

Publishing

Publishing means using your best handwriting to prepare a neat, error-free copy of your work so you can share it with others. Here are some ideas for publishing your writing about a journey.

• Write several more diary entries about your journey to complete a story. Make it into an illustrated book for your school library.
• Make your writing the first entry in a travel diary you plan to keep about real and imaginary journeys.
• Share your writing with a small group of classmates. Compare the diary entries to see how different writers imagined different kinds of journeys.

56

The Teacher Edition...streamlined instruction

At-a-glance stroke descriptions are short and easy to find.

Visual references to practice masters for each lesson save you time.

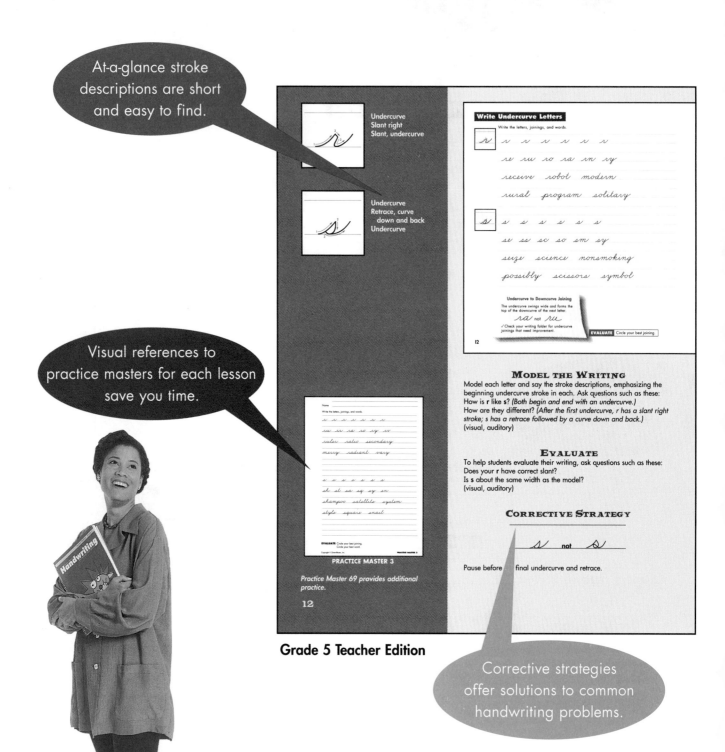

Grade 5 Teacher Edition

MODEL THE WRITING

Model each letter and say the stroke descriptions, emphasizing the beginning undercurve stroke in each. Ask questions such as these:
How is **r** like **s**? *(Both begin and end with an undercurve.)*
How are they different? *(After the first undercurve, r has a slant right stroke; s has a retrace followed by a curve down and back.)*
(visual, auditory)

EVALUATE

To help students evaluate their writing, ask questions such as these:
Does your **r** have correct slant?
Is **s** about the same width as the model?
(visual, auditory)

CORRECTIVE STRATEGY

Pause before the final undercurve and retrace.

Corrective strategies offer solutions to common handwriting problems.

The student page is close to the instruction for that page.

Language arts connections reinforce writing and other skills.

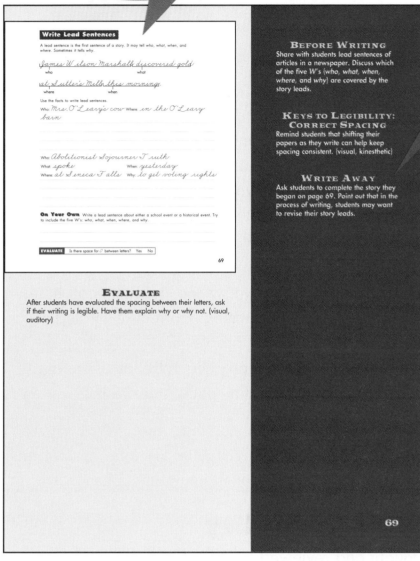

Grade 5 Teacher Edition

HANDWRITING AND THE WRITING PROCESS

Activities are suggested throughout the Teacher Edition that emphasize the importance of using legible handwriting in all the steps of the writing process.

MAINTAINING MANUSCRIPT

These activities emphasize the need for maintaining good manuscript in many situations throughout life, such as writing envelopes, job applications, test forms, and bank forms.

Grade 5 Practice Masters

An accompanying book of practice masters offers additional practice for every letter and skill students learn. It also includes resources to make teaching easier—certificates, an evaluation record, letters to send home to keep parents and guardians involved, and Spanish activities.

Evaluation and Assessment...
consistent guidance throughout the year

Student self-evaluation...

In every lesson. Students evaluate their own handwriting and circle their best work.

In every review. Several times a year, students review the letterforms and joinings they've learned and again evaluate their handwriting.

Through application activities. Students apply what they've learned in relevant practice activities that fill half the book. In each activity, they evaluate their own handwriting.

Teacher assessment...

In every lesson and review. As students evaluate their own writing, teachers can assess their letterforms, as well as their comprehension of good handwriting. Corrective Strategies for each lesson offer teachers helpful hints for common handwriting problems.

Through application activities. Students' work in relevant practice activities offers lots of opportunity for informal assessment of handwriting, language arts, and other areas.

The Keys to Legibility

These four Keys to Legibility are taught and reviewed throughout the program.
They remind students that their goal should be legible handwriting.

Size

Consistently sized letters are easy to read. Students learn to write letterforms that are consistent in size.

Slant

Letters with a consistent slant are easy to read. Students learn how to position their papers and hold their pencils so consistent slant comes with ease.

Shape

Four simple strokes—undercurve, downcurve, overcurve, and slant—make it easy for students to write letters with consistent and proper shape.

Spacing

Correct spacing between letters and words makes handwriting easy to read. Practical hints show students how to determine correct spacing.

Handwriting practice...relevant application

Write Quickly

Practice writing quickly. Choose one of these sayings from Ben Franklin's *Poor Richard's Almanac* or a favorite saying of your own. Write the sentence as many times as you can in one minute. At the same time, try to write legibly.

Fish and visitors smell in three days.
If your head is wax, don't walk in the sun.
A small leak will sink a great ship.

LEGIBLE LETTERS

Do not draw your letters.
Write smoothly.

See you later, alligator!
See you later, alligator!
See you later, alligator!
See you later, alligator!
See you later, alligator!
See you later, alligator!
See you later, alligator!

EVALUATE

Can you read your writing easily?	(Yes)	No
Can a friend read it?	(Yes)	No

48

**Completed Grade 5
Student Edition**

Students practice writing quickly and legibly, so their handwriting is very functional in the real world.

Edit Your Writing

Use these proofreading marks to edit your writing.

≡ Capitalize.	∧ Insert (add).
/ Use lowercase.	⋏ Delete (take out).
⊙ Add period.	¶ Indent for paragraph.

Write this paragraph correctly. Make the changes indicated by the proofreading marks.

¶ ~~You~~ Anyone can have a good time at a museum. Just follow ~~the~~ these Rules. Eat something ~~food~~ before you go. ≡ wear comfortable shoes. Don't try to see everything! Just pick ∧ one or two exhibits that interest you⊙

Anyone can have a good time at a museum. Just follow these rules. Eat something before you go. Wear comfortable shoes. Don't try to see everything! Just pick one or two exhibits that interest you.

EVALUATE | Does your writing have uniform slant? | (Yes) | No

61

In this practice activity, students learn how to edit and rewrite a paragraph.

A huge collection of supplementary materials... makes handwriting even easier to teach!

A **Evaluation Guides** *grades 1–6*

B **Poster/Wall Chart Super Pak**
grades K–6, includes Handwriting Positions
Wall Chart, Keys to Legibility Wall Chart,
Alphabet Wall Chart, Simplified Stroke
Descriptions, and a Portfolio Assessment Guide

C **Story Journals** *grades K–4*

D **Manuscript/Cursive Card Set** *grades 1–6*

E **Sentence Strips** *grades K–6*

F **Writing Journals** *grades 1–6*

G **My ABC Journal** *grades K–1*

H **Pignic Alphabet Book** *grades K–2*

I **From Anne to Zach Alphabet Book**
grades K–2

J **Letter Cards** *grades K–2*

K **Manuscript/Cursive Fonts**

L **Manuscript Kin-Tac Cards** *grades K–2*

For more information about these materials, call 1-800-421-3018.

- **M** **Make-Your-Own Big Book** *grades K–2*
- **N** **Parent Brochures** *for manuscript/cursive*
- **O** **Book of Transparencies** *grades 1–6*
- **P** **Read, Write, and Color Alphabet Mat** *grades K–2*
- **Q** **Dry Erase Write-On Cards** *grades K–2*
- **R** **Parent/Student Worksheets** *grades 2–6*
- **S** **Peek Thrus** *grades 1–4*

- **T** **Illustrated Alphabet Strips** *grades K–4*
- **U** **Desk Strips** *grades 1–6*
- **V** **Practice Masters** *grades K–6*
- **W** **Alphabet Wall Strips** *grades K–6*
- **X** **Fun With Handwriting** *grades K–8*
- **Y** **Write-On, Wipe-Off Magnetic Board With Letters** *grades K–2*
- **Z** **Post Office Kit** *grades K–4*

Vertical vs. *Slanted Manuscript*

What the research shows

Using a slanted alphabet has been a trend in handwriting instruction. It's actually not a new development—the first slanted alphabet was created in 1968. A sort of bridge between manuscript and cursive, this slanted alphabet used unconnected letterforms like the traditional vertical manuscript, but its letterforms were slanted like cursive.

It seemed like a good idea. This alphabet was to be easier to write than cursive, yet similar enough to cursive that children wouldn't learn two *completely* different alphabets. But after several years of use in some schools, research has uncovered some unfortunate findings.

Slanted manuscript can be difficult to write

Slanted manuscript was created to be similar to cursive, so it uses more complicated strokes such as small curves, and these strokes can be difficult for young children.

Vertical manuscript, on the other hand, is consistent with the development of young children. Each of its letters is formed with simple strokes—straight lines, circles, and slanted lines. One researcher found that the strokes used in vertical manuscript are the same as the shapes children use in their drawings (Farris, 1993). Because children are familiar with these shapes, they can identify and form the strokes with little difficulty.

Slanted manuscript can create problems with legibility

Legibility is an important goal in handwriting. Obviously, content should not be sacrificed for legibility, but what is handwriting if it cannot be read?

Educational researchers have tested the legibility of slanted manuscript and found that children writing vertical manuscript "performed significantly better" than those writing slanted manuscript. The writers of the slanted alphabet tended to make more misshapen letterforms, tended to extend their strokes above and below the guidelines, and had a difficult time keeping their letterforms consistent in size (Graham, 1992).

On the other hand, the vertical manuscript style of print has a lot of support in the area of research. Advertisers have known for years that italic type has a lower readability rate than vertical "roman" type. Research shows that in 30 minute readings, the italic style is read 4.9% slower than roman type (14–16 words per minute). This is why most literature, especially literature for early readers, is published using roman type.

Slanted manuscript can impair letter recognition

Educators have suspected that it would be beneficial for students to write and read the same style of alphabet. In other words, if children *read* vertical manuscript, they should also *write* vertical manuscript. Now it has been found that inconsistent alphabets may actually be detrimental to children's learning.

Researchers have found that slanted manuscript impairs the ability of some young children to recognize many letters. Some children who learn the slanted style alphabet find it difficult to recognize many of the traditional letterforms they see in books and environmental print. "[These children] consistently had difficulty identifying several letters, often making the same erroneous response to the same letter," the researchers reported. They concluded that slanted manuscript "creates substantially more

letter recognition errors and causes more letter confusion than does the traditional style." (Kuhl & Dewitz, 1994).

Slanted manuscript does not help with transition

One of the benefits proposed by the creators of the slanted manuscript alphabet was that it made it easier for children to make the transition from manuscript to cursive writing. However, no difference in transition time has been found between the two styles of manuscript alphabets. In addition, the slanted style does not seem to enhance young children's production of cursive letters (Graham, 1992).

"…slanted manuscript letters cannot be recommended as a replacement for the traditional manuscript alphabet."

The slanted style of manuscript appeared to be a good idea. But educators should take a close look at what the research shows before adopting this style of alphabet. As one researcher has said, "Given the lack of supportive evidence and the practical problems involved in implementation, slanted manuscript letters cannot be recommended as a replacement for the traditional manuscript alphabet" (Graham, 1994).

Farris, P.J. (1993). Learning to write the ABC's: A comparison of D'Nealian and Zaner-Bloser handwriting styles. *Indiana Reading Quarterly, 25* (4), 26–33.

Graham, S. (1992). Issues in handwriting instruction. *Focus on Exceptional Children, 25* (2).

Graham, S. (1994, Winter). Are slanted manuscript alphabets superior to the traditional manuscript alphabet? *Childhood Education,* 91–95.

Kuhl, D. & Dewitz, P. (1994, April). The effect of handwriting style on alphabet recognition. Paper presented at the annual meeting of the American Educational Research Association, New Orleans, LA.

Meeting Students' Individual Handwriting Needs

The Left-Handed Student

With proper instruction and encouragement, left-handed students can write as well as right-handed students. Three important techniques assist the left-handed student in writing.

Paper Position

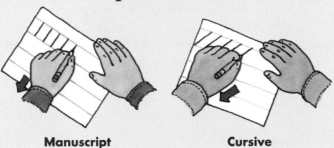

Manuscript   **Cursive**

For *manuscript writing*, the **lower right corner** of the paper should point toward the left of the body's mid-section.

For *cursive writing*, the **lower right corner** of the paper should point toward the body's midsection.

Downstrokes are pulled toward the left elbow.

Pencil Position

The top of the pencil should point toward the left elbow. The pen or pencil should be held at least one inch above the point. This allows students to see what they are writing.

Arm Position

Holding the left arm close to the body and keeping the hand below the line of writing prevents "hooking" the wrist and smearing the writing.

Students With Reversal Tendencies

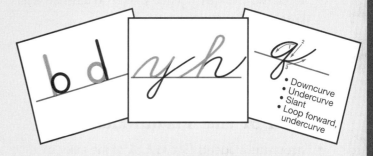

- Downcurve
- Undercurve
- Slant
- Loop forward, undercurve

Directionality

A problem with directionality (moving from left to right across the page) interferes with a child's ability to form letters correctly and to write text that makes sense. To develop correct directionality, try these techniques:

- Provide opportunities for the child to write at the chalkboard within a confined area with frequent arrows as a reminder of left-to-right progression.
- Prepare sheets of paper on which the left edges and the beginning stroke of a letter, such as *b*, are colored green.

Letter Reversals

Determine which letters a student most often reverses. Make a list of these reversals and concentrate on them either on an individual basis or by grouping together the students who are reversing the same letters.

- Emphasize each step of the stroke description before the children write a letter.
- Provide a letter for tracing that has been colored according to stroke order. Repeat the stroke description with the children as they write the letter.
- Encourage the children to write the letter as they verbalize the stroke description.

Students With Other Special Needs

Success in handwriting is almost always a certainty if the initial instruction involves visual, auditory, and kinesthetic stimuli—a multisensory approach. Students need to develop a correct mental and motor image of the stroke, joining, letter, or word before they attempt to write. These techniques may help your students with special needs.

For the Kinesthetic Learner

- Walk out the letter strokes on the floor.
- Form letters in the air using full-arm movement.
- Make letter models with clay or string.
- Write strokes, letters, and joinings in sand.
- Use different writing instruments, such as crayons, markers, and varied sizes of pencils.
- Trace large strokes, letters, and joinings on the chalkboard and on paper—first with fingers, then with chalk or other media.
- Dip fingers in water and form letters and joinings on the chalkboard.

Remember that initial instruction, remediation, and maintenance for the student whose primary sensory modality is kinesthetic should be tactile, involving movement and the sense of touch.

For the Auditory Learner

- Verbalize each stroke in the letter as that letter is presented.
- Encourage the student to verbalize the letter strokes and to explain how strokes are alike and how they are different in the letterforms.
- Ask students to write random letters as you verbalize the strokes.
- Be consistent in the language you use to describe letters, strokes, shapes, and joinings.

Students whose primary sensory modality is auditory require instruction that enables them to listen and to verbalize.

For the Visual Learner

- Encourage students first to look at the letter as a whole and to ask themselves if the letter is tall or short, fat or skinny. Does all of the letter rest on the baseline, or is it a descender or a tall letter? How many and what kinds of strokes are in the letter?
- Have students look at each individual stroke carefully before they attempt to write the letter.

As a general rule, a student whose primary sensory modality is visual will have little difficulty in handwriting if instruction includes adequate visual stimuli.

For Learners With Attention Deficit Problems

Because they have difficulty focusing and maintaining attention, these students must concentrate on individual strokes in the letterforms. When they have learned the strokes, they can put them together to form letters, and then learn the joinings (in cursive) to write words.

- Give very short assignments.
- Supervise closely and give frequent encouragement.

Activities recommended for kinesthetic learners are appropriate for students with an attention deficit disorder.

General Coaching Tips for Teachers

- Teach a handwriting lesson daily, if possible, for no more than 15 minutes. Short, daily periods of instruction are preferable to longer, but less frequent, periods.
- Surround children with models of good handwriting. Set an example when you write on the chalkboard and on students' papers.
- Teach the letters through basic strokes.
- Emphasize one key to legibility at a time.
- Use appropriately ruled paper. Don't be afraid to increase the size of the grids for any student who is experiencing difficulty.
- Stress comfortable writing posture and pencil position. Increase the size of the pencil for students who "squeeze" the writing implement.
- Show the alternate method of holding the pencil, and allow students to choose the one that is better for them. (Refer to the alternate method shown on the Position Pages in the Teacher Edition.)
- Provide opportunities for children in the upper grades to use manuscript writing. Permit manuscript for some assignments, if children prefer manuscript to cursive.
- Encourage students with poor sustained motor control to use conventional manuscript, with frequent lifts, if continuous manuscript is difficult for them.

Zaner-Bloser
Handwriting
With a simplified alphabet

Author
Clinton S. Hackney

Contributing Authors
Pamela J. Farris
Janice T. Jones
Linda Leonard Lamme

Zaner-Bloser, Inc.
P.O. Box 16764
Columbus, Ohio 43216-6764

Author
Clinton S. Hackney, Ed.D.

Contributing Authors
Pamela J. Farris, Ph.D.
Janice T. Jones, M.A.
Linda Leonard Lamme, Ph.D.

Reviewers
Judy L. Bausch, Columbus, Georgia
Cherlynn Bruce, Conroe, Texas
Karen H. Burke, Director of Curriculum and Instruction,
  Bar Mills, Maine
Anne Chamberlin, Lynchburg, Virginia
Carol J. Fuhler, Flagstaff, Arizona
Deborah G. Gallagher, Gainesville, Florida
Kathleen Harrington, Redford, Michigan
Rebecca James, East Greenbush, New York
Gerald R. Maeckelbergh, Principal, Blaine, Minnesota
Bessie B. Peabody, Principal, East St. Louis, Illinois

Marilyn S. Petruska, Coraopolis, Pennsylvania
Sharon Ralph, Nashville, Tennessee
Linda E. Ritchie, Birmingham, Alabama
Roberta Hogan Royer, North Canton, Ohio
Marion Redmond Starks, Baltimore, Maryland
Elizabeth J. Taglieri, Lake Zurich, Illinois
Claudia Williams, Lewisburg, West Virginia

Credits
Art: Marni Backer: 5, 78; Rosekrans Hoffman: 14, 24, 57, 67; Tom Leonard: 29, 32, 38, 60, 68; Diane Paterson: 52; Sarah Snow: 31, 36, 43, 44–45, 73, 77; Troy Viss: 25, 40, 41, 53, 70, 72, 74; Andrea Wallace: 4, 42, 46, 48

Photo: Hubert Manfred/Viesti Associates, *Dirt Road:* 54

Literature: "This Land Is Your Land." Words and Music by Woody Guthrie. TRO-© Copyright 1956 (Renewed), 1958 (Renewed) and 1970 Ludlow Music, Inc., New York, NY. Used by Permission.

Developed by Kirchoff/Wohlberg, Inc., in cooperation with Zaner-Bloser Publishers
Cover illustration by Lois Ehlert

ISBN 0-88085-950-4

CONTENTS

Did you know the word *cursive* comes from the Latin *currere*, which means "to run"? In this book, you'll "run" with cursive. After reviewing the strokes and letterforms, you'll improve your writing and pick up speed. You'll learn how to write quickly and legibly.

4

UNIT SUMMARY

This page tells students about the content, organization, and focus of the book. Students get started by taking a pretest to assess current ability. The lessons that follow review what students need to know to develop good handwriting skills.

PREVIEW THE BOOK

Preview the book with students, calling attention to its organization.

- Unit 1 presents handwriting basics.
- Unit 2 introduces lowercase and uppercase cursive letters grouped by common strokes.
- Unit 3 provides a variety of opportunities for students to write independently and to increase speed.

Point out that students will evaluate their handwriting frequently. Set up a portfolio for each student to assess individual progress throughout the year.

Pretest
This Land Is Your Land

This land is your land,
this land is my land
From California to the New York island,
From the redwood forest to the
Gulf Stream waters
This land was made for you and me.

As I was walking that ribbon of highway,
I saw above me that endless skyway,
I saw below me that golden valley
This land was made for you and me.

Woody Guthrie

On your paper, write the first stanza of this American folk song in your best cursive writing.

EVALUATE			
Are all your tall letters the same size?		Yes	No
Are your short letters half the height of your tall letters?		Yes	No
Did you avoid collisions?		Yes	No
Does your writing have uniform slant?		Yes	No
Is your spacing correct?		Yes	No

5

EVALUATE

As students write, monitor and informally assess their performance. Then guide them through the self-evaluation process. Meet individually with students to help them assess their handwriting. Ask them how they would like to improve their writing. (visual, auditory)

Have students use the first stanza of the folk song as a model for writing. Remind them to use correct letter size and shape, uniform slant, and correct spacing as they write. Tell students to place their pretests in their writing portfolios so they can write the same selection for the posttest later in the year. (visual, auditory, kinesthetic)

COACHING HINT: SELF-EVALUATION

Self-evaluation is an important step in the handwriting process. By identifying their own strengths and weaknesses, students become independent learners.

The steps in the self-evaluation process are as follows:

I. Question
Students should ask themselves questions such as these: "Is my slant correct?" "Do my letters rest on the baseline?"

2. Compare
Students should compare their handwriting to correct models.

3. Evaluate
Students should determine strengths and weaknesses in their handwriting based on the keys to legibility.

4. Diagnose
Students should diagnose the cause of any difficulties. Possible causes include incorrect paper or pencil position, inconsistent pressure on pencil, and incorrect strokes.

5. Improve
Self-evaluation should include a means of improvement through additional instruction and continued practice. (visual, auditory, kinesthetic)

Important Strokes for Cursive Writing

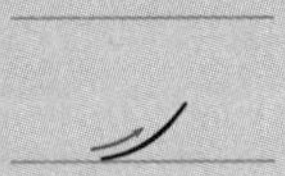

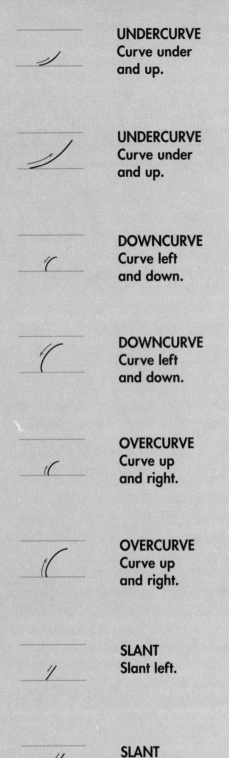

UNDERCURVE
Curve under and up.

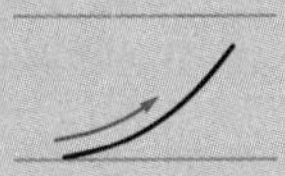

UNDERCURVE
Curve under and up.

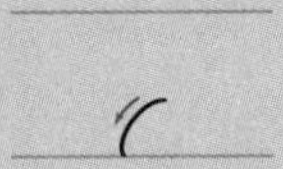

DOWNCURVE
Curve left and down.

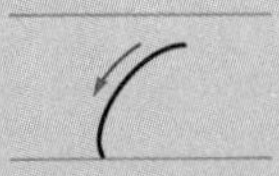

DOWNCURVE
Curve left and down.

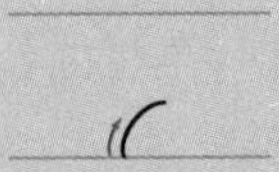

OVERCURVE
Curve up and right.

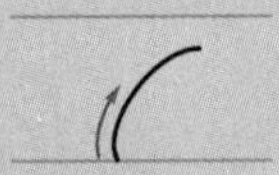

OVERCURVE
Curve up and right.

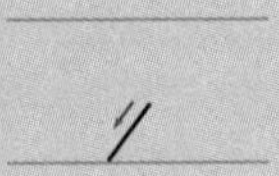

SLANT
Slant left.

SLANT
Slant left.

Coaching Hint

You may wish to group left-handed students together for instruction if you can do so without calling attention to the practice. They should be seated to the left of the chalkboard.

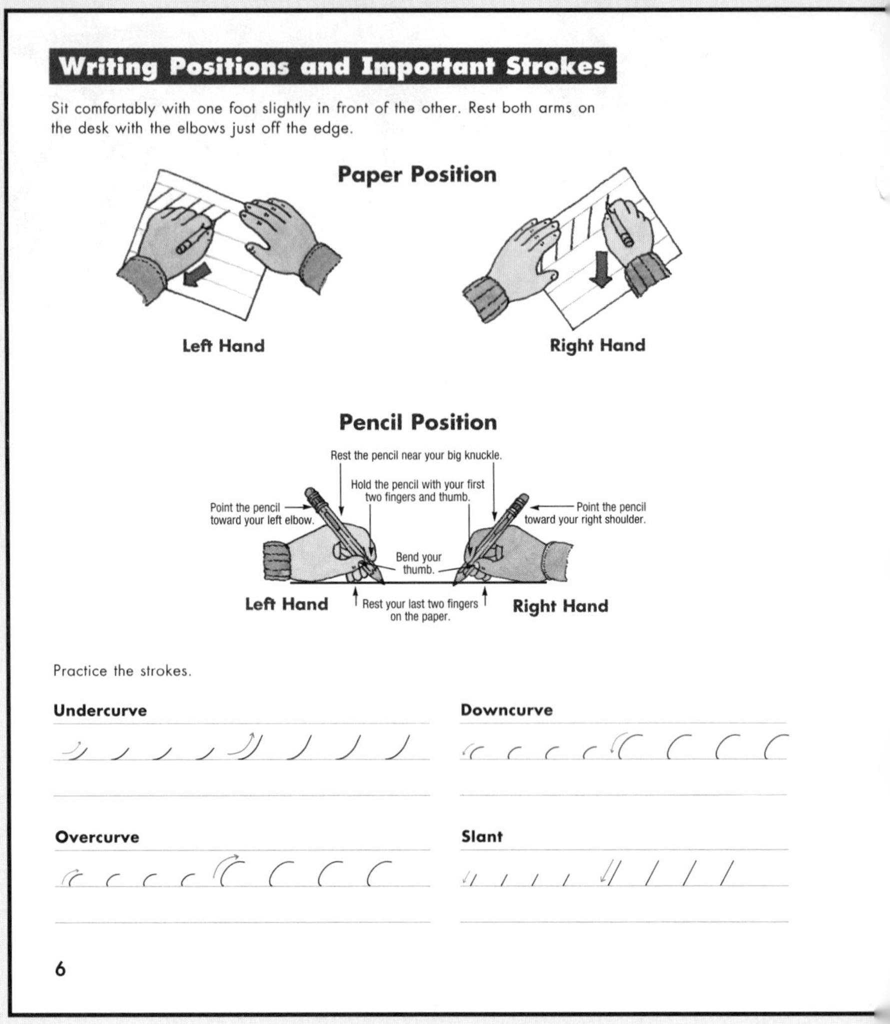

Writing Positions and Important Strokes

Sit comfortably with one foot slightly in front of the other. Rest both arms on the desk with the elbows just off the edge.

Paper Position

Left Hand

Right Hand

Pencil Position

Rest the pencil near your big knuckle.

Hold the pencil with your first two fingers and thumb.

Point the pencil toward your left elbow.

Point the pencil toward your right shoulder.

Bend your thumb.

Left Hand

Rest your last two fingers on the paper.

Right Hand

Practice the strokes.

Undercurve

Downcurve

Overcurve

Slant

6

Writing Positions

Suggest that students refer to this page throughout the year as a reminder of proper posture and correct paper and pencil position. Demonstrate correct positions for both left-handed and right-handed writers. Then ask students to place a sheet of paper in the proper position on their desks, pick up a pencil, and write their names. (visual, auditory, kinesthetic)

Model the Writing

Model the two sizes of each stroke on guidelines. Invite students to say the names as they write the strokes in the air. Point out that cursive letters are formed from these basic strokes. Suggest that students name the strokes as they write each letter to complete the page. (visual, auditory, kinesthetic)

Evaluate

Check for correct paper and pencil positions. The Zaner-Bloser Writing Frame can be used to improve hand position. (visual, kinesthetic)

Cursive Letters and Numerals

Aa Bb Cc Dd Ee Ff Gg
Hh Ii Jj Kk Ll Mm
Nn Oo Pp Qq Rr Ss Tt
Uu Vv Ww Xx Yy Zz
1 2 3 4 5 6 7 8 9 10

Write your initials, your nickname, and your full name.

_____

_____

Write your birth date and your age.

_____

Write the title of your favorite book or song.

_____

_____

Write the letters and numerals you want to improve.

_____

_____

7

EVALUATE

Poll students to find out which letters and numerals are most difficult for them to write. Discuss the problems students identify. (auditory)

CURSIVE LETTERS AND NUMERALS

Students can use the chart at the top of the page to review cursive letters and numerals. (visual, auditory)

COACHING HINT

Review with students the use of guidelines for correct letter formation. Draw guidelines on the chalkboard, and invite volunteers to write words on the guidelines. (visual, auditory, kinesthetic)

COACHING HINT: USE OF THE CHALKBOARD

You and your students can follow these suggestions for writing on the chalkboard.

Left-Hander. Stand in front of the writing lines and pull the downstrokes to the left elbow. The elbow is bent, and the writing is done at a comfortable height. Step to the right often to maintain correct slant.

Right-Hander. Stand to the left of the writing lines and pull the downstrokes toward the midsection of the body. The elbow is bent, and the writing is done at a comfortable height. Step to the right often to maintain correct slant. (visual, kinesthetic)

Students who have difficulty with the traditional pencil position may prefer the alternate method of holding the pencil between the first and second fingers.

UNIT SUMMARY

This lesson serves as an introduction to Unit 2. The lessons that follow emphasize cursive letter formation and joinings. Evaluations focus on letter size and shape.

PREVIEW THE UNIT

Preview the unit with students, calling attention to these features:

- letter models with numbered directional arrows
- guidelines for student writing directly beneath handwriting models
- reminders about joining letters
- geographical facts
- independent writing activities
- opportunities to evaluate letter size and shape

COACHING HINT

Demonstrate for students the technique of drawing a horizontal line with a ruler along the tops of their letters to show proper size. Have them practice this technique periodically to evaluate their letter size in curriculum areas that require handwriting, especially those that involve writing sentences or paragraphs. (visual, auditory, kinesthetic)

Keys to Legibility

To help make your writing legible, pay attention to size and shape, slant, and spacing.

Size and Shape

Tall letters should not touch the headline.

  Some lowercase letters are tall letters.

  All uppercase letters are tall letters.

  Numerals are the same height as tall letters.

b f t
a B C
1 2 3

Short letters should be half the height of tall letters.

  Some lowercase letters are short letters.

a g n

Descenders should not go too far below the baseline.

  Some lowercase letters have descenders.

  Some uppercase letters have descenders.

f g j
g y z

Write the words beneath the models. Pay careful attention to the size and shape of your letters.

legible   cursive   writing

communicate   penmanship

EVALUATE	Compare your words with the models.
	Are your letters the correct size and shape? Yes No

MODEL THE WRITING

Model writing a tall letter, a short letter, and a letter with a descender, noting the placement of each letter on the guidelines. Remind students that all letters of the same size should be the same height. (visual, auditory)

EVALUATE

Guide students through the self-evaluation process. Then ask if they can read their words easily. Encourage them to explain why or why not. (visual, auditory)

Slant

The slant of your writing should be uniform.

All your letters should slant forward.

dd dB db

Check the slant. Draw lines through the slant strokes of the letters.

Are your lines parallel?

Spacing

Your spacing should be correct.

between letters

between words

between sentences

letters

word word

end. Begin

Check the spacing. Write ⟋ between letters, ⟍ between words, and O between sentences.

Make sure your spacing is correct. Shift your paper as you write.

Write this sentence. Pay careful attention to slant and spacing.

This is my best handwriting.

EVALUATE	Does your writing have uniform slant?	Yes	No
	Is your spacing correct?	Yes	No

9

MODEL THE WRITING

To show an example of correct slant and spacing, write the following sentences on guidelines: *My writing is legible. The slant and the spacing are correct.* Invite students to check the slant by drawing lines through the slant strokes in the letters and to check the spacing by drawing ovals between letters, by drawing slanted lines between words, and by writing uppercase **O** between sentences. (visual, auditory, kinesthetic)

EVALUATE

Guide students through the self-evaluation process. Then ask them if they can read their sentences easily. Encourage them to explain why or why not. (visual, auditory)

HANDWRITING AND THE WRITING PROCESS

Throughout this unit, statements preceded by a red check mark will prompt students to go to their writing folders and check for joinings that need improvement. If cumulative folders are not available, students may evaluate any written work (including homework papers, tests, and creative writing assignments).

You may wish to take these opportunities to remind students that legible handwriting is important in all subject areas. Getting into the habit of evaluating handwriting as a regular part of the editing stage of the writing process will help students maintain their handwriting skills.

Undercurve
Slant, undercurve,
    (lift)
Dot

Undercurve
Slant, undercurve,
    (lift)
Slide right

Write Undercurve Letters

Write the letters, joinings, and words.

i   *i   i   i   i   i   i*

ir   ie   id   ia   im   iv

irregular   idle   important

libraries   inertia   civilize

t   *t   t   t   t   t   t*

tr   te   to   ta   ty   tm

traveler   topic   type

territory   attack   treatment

Undercurve to Undercurve Joining

The undercurve ending swings wide directly
into the undercurve of the following letter.

ie not *ll*

✓Check your writing folder for undercurve
joinings that need improvement.

EVALUATE Circle your best joining.

10

Practice Master

Name _____

Write the letters, joinings, and words.

i   i   i   i   i   i   i

is   ir   ig   ia   in   im

misjudge   delight   instant

circuit   digit   imitate

t   t   t   t   t   t

th   tf   ta   to   tm   ty

through   tax   appointment

tactful   together   typist

EVALUATE Circle your best joining.
              Circle your best word.

Copyright © Zaner-Bloser, Inc.

PRACTICE MASTER I

PRACTICE MASTER I

Practice Master 67 provides additional practice.

MODEL THE WRITING

Model each letter and say the stroke descriptions, emphasizing the beginning undercurve stroke in each. Ask questions such as these:
In what ways are the letters alike? *(They begin with undercurve, slant, undercurve.)*
What size is **t**? *(tall)*
(visual, auditory)

EVALUATE

To help students evaluate their writing, ask questions such as these:
Did you pull the slant strokes to the baseline?
Is **t** crossed correctly?
Does **i** rest on the baseline?
(visual, auditory)

CORRECTIVE STRATEGY

i not *i*

Pull the slant stroke to the baseline.

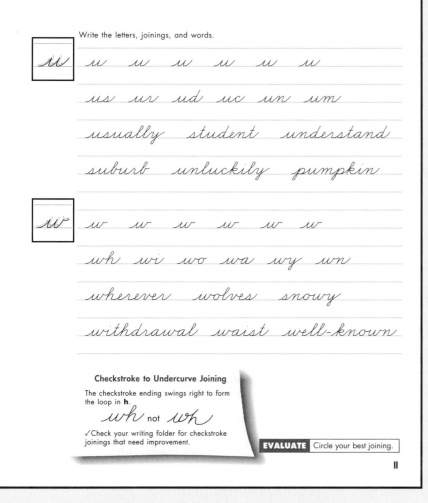

Write the letters, joinings, and words.

u u u u u u u

us ur ud uc un um

usually student understand

suburb unluckily pumpkin

w w w w w w

wh wi wo wa wy wn

wherever wolves snowy

withdrawal waist well-known

Checkstroke to Undercurve Joining

The checkstroke ending swings right to form the loop in **h**.

wh not *wh*

✓Check your writing folder for checkstroke joinings that need improvement.

EVALUATE Circle your best joining.

ll

Undercurve
Slant, undercurve
Slant, undercurve

Undercurve
Slant, undercurve
Slant, undercurve
Checkstroke

MODEL THE WRITING

Model each letter and say the stroke descriptions, emphasizing the beginning undercurve stroke in each. Ask questions such as these:

How many slant strokes are in **u**? *(two)*

Which letter ends with a checkstroke? *(w)*

How is **w** like **u**? *(Both begin with undercurve, slant, undercurve.)* (visual, auditory)

EVALUATE

To help students evaluate their writing, ask questions such as these:

Did you pull the slant strokes to the baseline?

Are the slant strokes in **u** and **w** parallel?

Do your letters rest on the baseline?

(visual, auditory)

CORRECTIVE STRATEGY

w **not** *u*

Retrace only slightly before swinging right.

PRACTICE MASTER 2

Practice Master 68 provides additional practice.

11

Undercurve
Slant right
Slant, undercurve

Undercurve
Retrace, curve
down and back
Undercurve

Practice Master 69 provides additional practice.

Write Undercurve Letters

Write the letters, joinings, and words.

r   *r r r r r r*

re ru ro ra rn ry

receive robot modern

rural program solitary

s   *s s s s s s*

se ss sc so sm sy

seize science nonsmoking

possibly scissors symbol

Undercurve to Downcurve Joining

The undercurve swings wide and forms the top of the downcurve of the next letter.

ra not *ru*

✓Check your writing folder for undercurve joinings that need improvement.

EVALUATE Circle your best joining.

12

MODEL THE WRITING

Model each letter and say the stroke descriptions, emphasizing the beginning undercurve stroke in each. Ask questions such as these:
How is **r** like **s**? *(Both begin and end with an undercurve.)*
How are they different? *(After the first undercurve, r has a slant right stroke; s has a retrace followed by a curve down and back.)*
(visual, auditory)

EVALUATE

To help students evaluate their writing, ask questions such as these:
Does your **r** have correct slant?
Is **s** about the same width as the model?
(visual, auditory)

CORRECTIVE STRATEGY

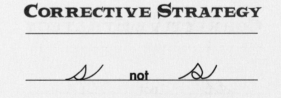

Pause before the final undercurve and retrace.

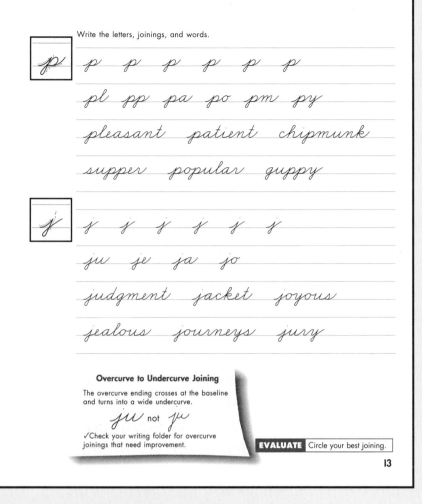

Write the letters, joinings, and words.

p p p p p p p

pl pp pa po pm py

pleasant patient chipmunk

supper popular guppy

j j j j j j j

ju je ja jo

judgment jacket joyous

jealous journeys jury

Overcurve to Undercurve Joining

The overcurve ending crosses at the baseline and turns into a wide undercurve.

ju not *ju*

✓Check your writing folder for overcurve joinings that need improvement.

EVALUATE Circle your best joining.

13

Undercurve
Slant, loop back
Overcurve, curve
    back
Undercurve

Undercurve
Slant
Loop back,
    overcurve, (lift)
Dot

MODEL THE WRITING

Model each letter and say the stroke descriptions, emphasizing the beginning undercurve stroke in each. Ask questions such as these:
Which letter begins and ends with an undercurve? *(p)*
Which letter ends with an overcurve? *(j)*
(visual, auditory)

EVALUATE

To help students evaluate their writing, ask questions such as these:
Do the loops of your **p** and **j** close at the baseline?
Are the strokes smooth and even?
(visual, auditory)

CORRECTIVE STRATEGY

j not *j*

Cross the overcurve at the baseline.

Name _____

Write the letters, joinings, and words.

p p p p p p

pr pe po pa py pm

prison position pyramid

perpendicular paid chipmunk

j j j j j j

je ju ji ja jo

jewelry jingle janitor

justice pajamas joyful

EVALUATE Circle your best joining.
Circle your best word.

PRACTICE MASTER 4

Copyright © Zaner-Bloser, Inc.

PRACTICE MASTER 4

Practice Master 70 provides additional practice.

13

Write the undercurve letters **i, t, u, w, r, s, p,** and **j** as you say the stroke descriptions. Review the undercurve to undercurve, overcurve to undercurve, and checkstroke to undercurve joinings (**it, ju, wr**).

Pair students and give them a two-minute period to write quickly but legibly as many words as possible containing **it, ju,** and **wr.** Ask volunteers to write their lists of words on the chalkboard, paying close attention to forming and joining the letters correctly. (visual, auditory, kinesthetic)

COACHING HINT

Keep a record of the letters students are having problems with. Provide practice with these letters by assigning writing exercises such as making word lists and writing tongue twisters. (visual, auditory, kinesthetic)

WRITE AWAY

Ask students to make their own classification worksheets. Suggest they add *Mineral* to the categories *Animal* and *Vegetable* or use different categories, such as *People, Places,* and *Things.*

14

Review

Sort the words. Write each one in the correct category.
Use a dictionary to check word meanings.

ultrasaurus   ibis   shallot   lentil
rutabaga   parsnip   jicama   rhea
watermelon   rhubarb   jaguar   sloth
terrapin   platypus   taro   wombat

Animal	Vegetable
ultrasaurus	rutabaga
terrapin	watermelon
ibis	parsnip
platypus	rhubarb
jaguar	shallot
rhea	jicama
sloth	taro
wombat	lentil

On Your Own Add four words of your own to the chart.

EVALUATE	Did you join your letters correctly?	Yes	No
	Did you close each *s, p,* and *j*?	Yes	No

14

EVALUATE

Guide students through the self-evaluation process, focusing on letter formation and joinings. Encourage students to explain why one letter or joining they wrote might be better than another. (visual, auditory)

Writing Legibly

1. Study these tips for legible writing. They will help you avoid common handwriting errors when you write.

✓ Don't loop non-looped letters. Write *t*, not *t*.

✓ Make sure undercurves rest on the baseline. Write *u*, not *u*.

✓ When letters have loops that go below the baseline, close the loop at the baseline. Write *p*, not *p*.

✓ Keep your slant consistent. Write *u*, not *u*.

2. Look at these words from a student's spelling list. Underline letters that need improvement.

impolite   *weather*
peanut butter   *splatter*
project   *statue*
shipwreck   *jewelry*

3. Rewrite the spelling words correctly, or write some of your own spelling or vocabulary words. Pay attention to the tips for legible writing.

_____   _____

_____   _____

_____   _____

_____   _____

EVALUATE			
Is each non-looped letter written without a loop?		Yes	No
Do your undercurves rest on the baseline?		Yes	No
Did you close the loop at the baseline in letters like *p* and *f*?		Yes	No
Is your slant consistent?		Yes	No

15

Downcurve
Undercurve
Slant, undercurve

Downcurve
Undercurve

Downcurve
Undercurve
Slant, undercurve

Practice Masters 71 and 72 provide additional practice.

Write Downcurve Letters

Write the letters, joinings, and words.

a | a a a a a a

al ai ac ag am az

aloud   almanac   amaze

c | c c c c c c

ci cl co cc cy cz

vaccine   concert   bicycle

d | d d d d d d

di de da do dv dm

diameter   daisies   advertise

Undercurve to Overcurve Joining

The undercurve ending swings wide, then overcurves quickly into the slant stroke.

am not am

✓Check your writing folder for undercurve joinings that need improvement.

EVALUATE | Circle your best joining.

16

MODEL THE WRITING

Model each letter and say the stroke descriptions, emphasizing the downcurve stroke in each. Ask questions such as these:
How are **a** and **d** alike? *(They have the same strokes.)*
What strokes are they? *(downcurve, undercurve, slant, undercurve)*
How does **c** end? *(with an undercurve)*
(visual, auditory)

EVALUATE

To help students evaluate their writing, ask questions such as these:
Do your letters have correct slant?
Did you pull the slant strokes in **a** and **d** to the baseline?
(visual, auditory)

CORRECTIVE STRATEGY

a **not** a

Pause after the first undercurve, then pull the slant stroke to the baseline.

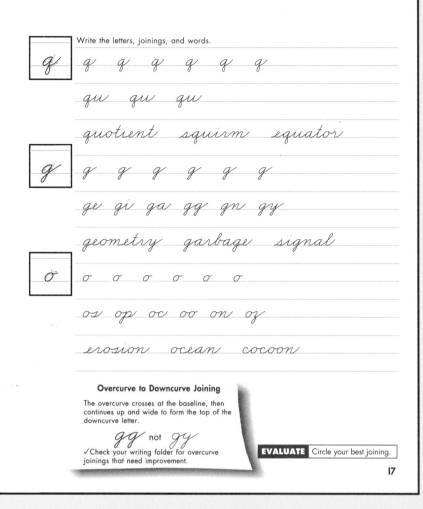

Write the letters, joinings, and words.

q q q q q q

qu qu qu

quotient squirm equator

g g g g g g

ge gi ga gg gn gy

geometry garbage signal

o o o o o o

os op oc oo on oz

erosion ocean cocoon

Overcurve to Downcurve Joining

The overcurve crosses at the baseline, then continues up and wide to form the top of the downcurve letter.

gg not gy

✓Check your writing folder for overcurve joinings that need improvement.

EVALUATE Circle your best joining.

17

Downcurve
Undercurve
Slant
Loop forward,
  undercurve

Downcurve
Undercurve
Slant
Loop back,
  overcurve

Downcurve
Undercurve
Checkstroke

MODEL THE WRITING

Model each letter and say the stroke descriptions, emphasizing the downcurve stroke in each. Ask questions such as these:
How does **g** differ from **q**? *(While g loops back and ends with an overcurve, q loops forward and ends with an undercurve.)*
How does **o** end? *(with a checkstroke)*
(visual, auditory)

EVALUATE

To help students evaluate their writing, ask questions such as these:
Do your letters have correct slant?
Do the loops of your **q** and **g** close at the baseline?
(visual, auditory)

CORRECTIVE STRATEGY

o **not** *o*

Make a wide downcurve beginning.

PRACTICE MASTER 6

Practice Masters 72 and 73 provide additional practice.

17

Overcurve, slant
Overcurve, slant
Undercurve

Overcurve, slant
Overcurve, slant
Overcurve, slant
Undercurve

Overcurve, slant
Undercurve, (lift)
Slant

Write Overcurve Letters

Write the letters, joinings, and words.

n

n n n n n n

nt ni no nc nn nm

prevent nonmetal pennies

m

m m m m m m

mi me ma mo mm my

midair margin midsummer

x

x x x x x x

xp xi xe xc xa xy

explained excellent waxy

Undercurve to Downcurve Joining

The undercurve swings up and over to form
the top of the downcurve letter. Remember to
cross **x** after the word is finished.

xc not xc

✓Check your writing folder for undercurve
joinings that need improvement.

EVALUATE Circle your best joining.

18

Name _____

Write the letters, joinings, and words.

n n n n n n n

ne ni nd nc ny nn

neutral sandwich funny

m m m m m m m

me mb mo ma my mm

member motivate balmy

x x x x x x x

xe xp xi xc xa xy

exercise excite galaxy

EVALUATE Circle your best joining.
Circle your best word.

Copyright © Zaner-Bloser, Inc.   **PRACTICE MASTER 7**

PRACTICE MASTER 7

Practice Masters 74 and 75 provide
additional practice.

18

MODEL THE WRITING

Model each letter and say the stroke descriptions, emphasizing the
beginning overcurve stroke in each. Ask questions such as these:
How do all the letters begin? *(with overcurve, slant)*
Which letter has a lift? *(x)*
(visual, auditory)

EVALUATE

To help students evaluate their writing, ask questions such as these:
Are your overcurves round?
Are your slant strokes pulled to the baseline?
Is your **x** crossed in the middle of the slant stroke?
(visual, auditory)

CORRECTIVE STRATEGY

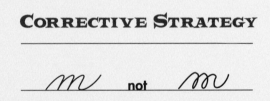

m not m

Pause after the first two slant strokes.

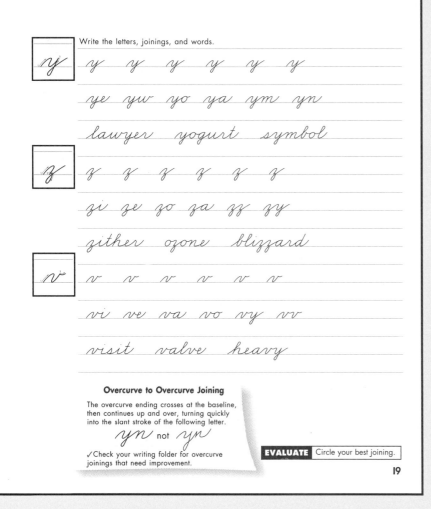

Write the letters, joinings, and words.

y *y* *y* *y* *y* *y* *y*

ye *yw* *yo* *ya* *ym* *yn*

lawyer *yogurt* *symbol*

z *z* *z* *z* *z* *z*

zi *ze* *zo* *za* *zz* *zy*

zither *ozone* *blizzard*

v *v* *v* *v* *v* *v*

vi *ve* *va* *vo* *vy* *vv*

visit *valve* *heavy*

Overcurve to Overcurve Joining

The overcurve ending crosses at the baseline, then continues up and over, turning quickly into the slant stroke of the following letter.

yn not *yn*

✓Check your writing folder for overcurve joinings that need improvement.

EVALUATE Circle your best joining.

19

Overcurve, slant
Undercurve
Slant
Loop back,
    overcurve

Overcurve, slant
Overcurve
Curve down
Loop, overcurve

Overcurve, slant
Undercurve
Checkstroke

MODEL THE WRITING

Model each letter and say the stroke descriptions, emphasizing the beginning overcurve stroke in each. Ask questions such as these:
How many overcurves are in **y**? *(two)*
Which letters end with an overcurve? *(y, z)*
Which letter ends with a checkstroke? *(v)*
(visual, auditory)

EVALUATE

To help students evaluate their writing, ask questions such as these:
Is each letter about the same width as the model?
Does your **v** end with a checkstroke?
(visual, auditory)

CORRECTIVE STRATEGY

y not *y*

Position paper properly.

PRACTICE MASTER 8

Practice Masters 75 and 76 provide additional practice.

REFOCUS

Refer students to the cursive alphabet on page 7. Ask them to locate the six lowercase letters that begin with a downcurve (**a, c, d, q, g, o**) and the six lowercase letters that begin with an overcurve (**n, m, x, y, z, v**). Invite volunteers to write each letter on the chalkboard and name the ending stroke.

Have students write various combinations of three of the twelve letters on the chalkboard as they identify the joining strokes. Students can use colored chalk to highlight the joinings. (visual, auditory, kinesthetic)

COACHING HINT

Remind students that a little more space is needed before words that begin with a downcurve letter (**a, c, d, q, g, o**). Write a sentence on the chalkboard, for example, *An alligator gave the ducks quite a scare.* Use colored chalk to indicate where more space is needed. (visual, auditory)

WRITE AWAY

Ask students to write sentences using three related compound words from page 20. Participate by sharing sentences with students.

Review

air   cat   day   extra   golden   moon
night   out   quick   video   yard   zero

Choose and write a word that goes with each set of words.
Use a dictionary if you need help.

break	dream	time	*day*
club	fall	gown	night
line	mail	port	air
sand	silver	step	quick
field	fit	law	out
rod	rule	wedding	golden
cassette	phone	tape	video
beam	light	walk	moon
ordinary	sensory	terrestrial	extra
bird	call	tail	cat
hour	gravity	in on	zero
line	sale	stick	yard

On Your Own Write three words that go with the word *down*.

EVALUATE	Did you join your letters correctly?	Yes	No
	Do your letters have uniform slant?	Yes	No

20

EVALUATE

Guide students through the self-evaluation process, focusing on letter slant and joinings. Encourage students to explain why one letter or joining they wrote might be better than another. (visual, auditory)

Writing Legibly

1. Study these tips for legible writing. They will help you avoid common handwriting errors when you write.

✓ Close letters that should be closed. Write *d*, not *cl*.

✓ Keep checkstrokes at the right height. Write *o*, not *a*.

✓ Make sure curves are smooth and rounded. Write *m*, not *M*.

✓ Begin overcurve letters with an overcurve. Write *v*, not *u*.

2. Look at this student's math story problem. Underline letters that need improvement.

> Ryan invited sixteen friends
> to a mid-week pizza party. Each
> pizza has eight slices. How many
> pizzas are needed so that the
> serving for each guest equals four
> slices?

3. Rewrite the problem correctly, or write a math story problem of your own. Pay attention to the tips for legible writing.

EVALUATE			
Did you close letters that should be closed?	Yes	No	
Are checkstrokes at the right height?	Yes	No	
Did you write smooth, rounded curves?	Yes	No	
Do your overcurve letters begin with an overcurve?	Yes	No	

21

BEFORE WRITING

Discuss the importance of legible writing in all areas of the school curriculum. Talk about how illegible writing may affect the outcome of a story problem.

COACHING HINT

Encourage students to look through their writing folders or other school papers and select a sample that best showcases their ability to write legibly. Students may change their selections as their handwriting skills improve. (visual, kinesthetic)

EVALUATE

Guide students through the evaluation process, focusing on the featured tips for legible writing. You may wish to add to a list of tips to be displayed permanently in your classroom. (visual, auditory)

Undercurve
Loop back, slant
Undercurve

Undercurve
Loop back, slant
Undercurve

Undercurve
Loop back, slant
Overcurve, slant
Undercurve

Write Letters With Loops

Write the letters, joinings, and words.

e   e   e   e   e   e   e

ei   el   ed   ea   em   ex

eighty   excited   element

l   l   l   l   l   l

ll   ls   lo   la   ly   lm

balloon   loudly   lying

h   h   h   h   h   h

hi   ht   ha   ho   hy   hm

historic   handsome   rhythm

Undercurve to Undercurve Joining

The undercurve joining must be wide to allow room for the loop in **l**.

kl not kl

✓Check your writing folder for undercurve joinings that need improvement.

EVALUATE Circle your best joining.

22

MODEL THE WRITING

Model each letter and say the stroke descriptions, emphasizing the beginning loop in each. Ask questions such as these:
In what ways are the letters alike? *(They begin with undercurve, loop back, and slant; they end with an undercurve.)*
Which letters are tall? *(l, h)*
(visual, auditory)

EVALUATE

To help students evaluate their writing, ask questions such as these:
Are all your letters the correct size?
Did you pull the slant strokes to the baseline?
Are your strokes smooth and even?
(visual, auditory)

CORRECTIVE STRATEGY

l   not   l

Begin the last undercurve at the baseline and end at the top of the letter.

Name _____

Write the letters, joinings, and words.

e e e e e e

el ei ea eo en ex

elevator easy entrance

l l l l l l

le ll la lo lm ly

legend latest calmly

h h h h h h

he ht ho ha hm hy

health hobbies birthmark

EVALUATE Circle your best joining.
        Circle your best word.

Copyright © Zaner-Bloser, Inc.

PRACTICE MASTER 9

PRACTICE MASTER 9

Practice Masters 77 and 78 provide additional practice.

22

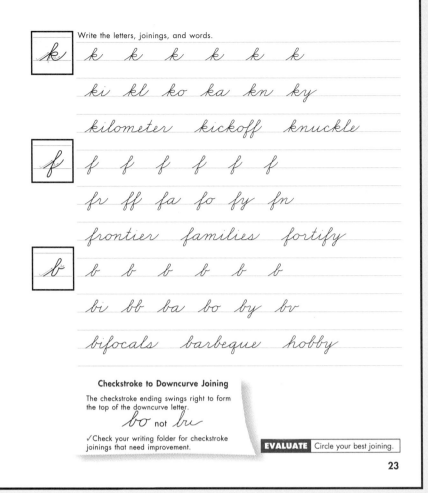

Write the letters, joinings, and words.

k k k k k k k

ki kl ko ka kn ky

kilometer kickoff knuckle

f f f f f f

fr ff fa fo fy fn

frontier families fortify

b b b b b b

bi bb ba bo by br

bifocals barbeque hobby

Checkstroke to Downcurve Joining
The checkstroke ending swings right to form
the top of the downcurve letter.

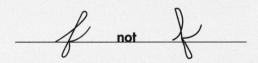

bo not bu

✓Check your writing folder for checkstroke
joinings that need improvement.

EVALUATE Circle your best joining.

23

Undercurve
Loop back, slant
Overcurve, curve
    forward, curve
        under
Slant right,
    undercurve

Undercurve
Loop back, slant
Loop forward
Undercurve

Undercurve
Loop back, slant
Undercurve
Checkstroke

MODEL THE WRITING

Model each letter and say the stroke descriptions, emphasizing the
beginning loop in each. Ask questions such as these:
How are **k** and **f** alike? *(Both begin and end with an undercurve.)*
How does **b** end? *(with a checkstroke)*
(visual, auditory)

EVALUATE

To help students evaluate their writing, ask questions such as these:
Is the forward curve of your **k** closed?
Does the lower loop of your **f** close at the baseline?
Are all your letters the correct size?
(visual, auditory)

CORRECTIVE STRATEGY

f not f

Position paper properly, pull the slant stroke to the baseline.

Name _____

Write the letters, joinings, and words.

k k k k k k k

ke kl ka kd ky kn

keynote karate skyscraper

f f f f f f f

fl ff fa fo fy fn

fluoride fashion classify

b b b b b b b

bu bb bo ba by br

busily billboard nearby

EVALUATE Circle your best joining.
Circle your best word.

PRACTICE MASTER 10   Copyright © Zaner-Bloser, Inc.

PRACTICE MASTER 10

*Practice Masters 78 and 79 provide
additional practice.*

REFOCUS

Write the six letters with loops (**e, l, h, k, f, b**). Ask students to think of words spelled with one or more of these letters. Write their responses, incorrectly closing the loops in some of the letters.

Ask students to locate, describe, and correct the errors. Have students name the strokes as they form the letters with loops. (visual, auditory, kinesthetic)

COACHING HINT

Students' progress in handwriting is greater when short, intensive periods of instruction are used. Fifteen minutes for a lesson is optimal.

WRITE AWAY

Challenge students to write riddles for homophone pairs. Participate by providing an example, such as *What do you call the main rule of conduct? (the principal principle)*

Review

beagle	billy	bog	deer
fake	frog	glen	goose
hawk	hen	legal	loose
silly	snake	spear	talk

Choose and write a pair of rhyming words to answer each question.

silly billy

Question	Word 1	Word 2
What is a foolish male goat?	silly	billy
What is a valley for female fowls?	hen	glen
What is conversation among birds of prey?	hawk	talk
What is a runaway bird?	loose	goose
What is a home for amphibians?	frog	bog
What is a synthetic boa?	fake	snake
What is a dog with a license?	legal	beagle
What is a buck's antler?	deer	spear

On Your Own Write a question about a pair of rhyming words. Ask a friend to answer it.

EVALUATE Are the loops in each *e, l, h, k, f,* and *b* open?   Yes   No

24

EVALUATE

Guide students through the self-evaluation process, focusing on letter formation. Encourage students to explain why one letter they wrote might be better than another. (visual, auditory)

24

Manuscript Maintenance

The Hawaiian alphabet has only these twelve letters.

a e i o u h k l m n p w

Use these letters to form as many words as you can. Write in lowercase manuscript.

EVALUATE Are your letters formed correctly? Yes No

DID YOU KNOW The Hawaiian alphabet also has a symbol ʻ called "Okina."

25

On the chalkboard, write this sentence in manuscript: *E'olelo Hawai'i wale no ma 'ane'i.* (Only Hawaiian spoken here.) Point out that Hawaii is the only state that has two official languages: English and Hawaiian.

MANUSCRIPT MAINTENANCE

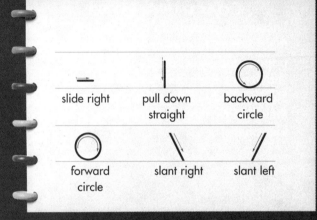

| slide right | pull down straight | backward circle |
| forward circle | slant right | slant left |

Review the basic strokes for manuscript writing. Remind students that all manuscript letters are formed with these strokes and that manuscript writing is vertical. Have students practice the strokes and letterforms. Tell them to adjust the position of the paper for manuscript writing. (visual, auditory, kinesthetic)

WRITE AWAY

Ask students to use the first thirteen letters of the alphabet to write as many words as they can. Have students write in lowercase manuscript.

COACHING HINT

To reinforce manuscript writing, have students use manuscript to prepare invitations to parties, to send holiday greetings, and to label maps and diagrams.

Practice Masters 58–65 provide manuscript writing practice.

25

EVALUATE

Have students focus on size and shape to determine whether their lowercase manuscript letters are legible. Discuss ways to improve legibility. (visual, auditory)

 ### MAINTAINING MANUSCRIPT

Permit students to use manuscript for creative writing, spelling assignments, and tests if they choose to do so.

Give a weekly assignment that requires manuscript, such as filling out forms, map study, charts, preparing labels and captions, crossword puzzles, and making posters.

Use manuscript on the chalkboard for various purposes, especially vocabulary and dictionary study, as well as other work involving word attack skills.

Discuss the importance of legible writing in all areas of the school curriculum. Talk about how the ability to write legibly allows a writer to focus more on the content of his or her story. Preview the three steps on pages 26 and 27 and explain that following them is a good strategy to use as a part of a regular writing routine.

COACHING HINT

Encourage students to look through their writing folders or other school papers and select a sample that best showcases their ability to write legibly. Students may change their selections as their handwriting skills improve. (visual, kinesthetic)

Writing Legibly

When you edit and proofread your writing, do you remember to check your handwriting? Taking time to make sure your handwriting is legible shows courtesy to your readers. It also helps you keep your handwriting skills sharp. Follow these steps for writing legibly.

1. **Study** tips for legible writing. The **Keys to Legibility** are easy to remember. They tell you what qualities to look for in your handwriting.

   ✓ Each letter should have good **shape**.
   Write *b*, not *b*. Write *e*, not *e*.

   ✓ Make sure letters are the right **size**. Tall letters should be twice the height of short letters.
   Write *l*, not *l*.

   ✓ Keep your **slant** consistent.
   Write *f*, not *f*.

   ✓ Check for good **spacing**. Leave space for *o* between letters, space for \ between words, and space for *O* between sentences.
   Write *Check the chalkboard*, not *Check the chalkboard*.

2. **Look** closely at your writing. To practice, underline places that need improvement in this student's story beginning.

   A rainy day found my cousin Robin and me stuck inside at our aunt's house. We got bored just hanging around playing video games. "Let's explore the basement of this old house," Robin said. I agreed. Down the damp, crumbling steps we went, brushing cobwebs from our faces. Thick dust lay over boxes, jars, and strange artifacts stacked on leaning shelves.

26

EVALUATE

Guide students through the process of evaluating the sample student writing, focusing on the Keys to Legibility. You may wish to add to a list of tips for legible writing to be displayed permanently in your classroom. (visual, auditory)

"Hey, what's this?" Robin shouted, making my shoulders shake with fright.

"It looks like a door," I said as I knelt to open the rotting square of wood on rusty hinges.

"It's some kind of passageway," Robin guessed. "Let's check it out."

3. **Rewrite,** correcting the mistakes you found. On the lines below, rewrite the story beginning, continue the story, or write a story of your own.

_____

_____

_____

_____

_____

_____

_____

_____

_____

_____

_____

EVALUATE			
Does each letter have good **shape**?		Yes	No
Are tall letters twice the **size** of short letters?		Yes	No
Did you write with consistent **slant**?		Yes	No
Is there good **spacing** between letters, words, and sentences?		Yes	No

WRITE AWAY
Work as a class to brainstorm ideas for completing the story begun on page 26. Focus on the Keys to Legibility as you work together to write the finished story on chart paper or an overhead projector. (visual, kinesthetic)

EVALUATE
Guide students in using the Keys to Legibility to evaluate their writing. Ask volunteers to explain specific changes they made during rewriting. (visual, auditory)

Downcurve
Undercurve
Slant, undercurve

Slant
Downcurve
Undercurve

Write Downcurve Letters

Write the letters, joinings, and words. Then write the sentence.

a   *a a a a a a*

Al Ar Ac Ag An Am

Alaska   Acapulco   Anchorage

C   *C C C C C C*

Cl Ch Ca Co Cy Cz

Cleveland   Canada   Cyprus

DID YOU KNOW?

Camellias grow in Alabama.

EVALUATE Circle your best joining.

28

Name _____

a and *C* are joined to the letter that follows.
Write the letters, joinings, and words. Then write the sentence.

a a a a a a a

Au Ar Ad Ac Am An

Australia Aden America

Chester A. Arthur Akron

C C C C C C

Ch Cv Co Ca Cy Cz

Chicago Colombia Cyrene

Calvin Coolidge Columbus

DID YOU KNOW?

Australia is a continent.

EVALUATE Circle your best joining.
Circle your best word.

PRACTICE MASTER 13

PRACTICE MASTER 13

Practice Master 81 provides additional practice.

MODEL THE WRITING

Model each letter and say the stroke descriptions, emphasizing the downcurve stroke in each. Ask questions such as these:
Which letter begins with a downcurve? *(A)*
How does **C** begin? *(with a slant)*
(visual, auditory)

EVALUATE

To help students evaluate their writing, ask questions such as these:
Is your **A** closed?
Does your **C** have correct slant?
(visual, auditory)

CORRECTIVE STRATEGY

a not *a*

Make a wide downcurve beginning.

Write the letters, joinings, and words. Then write the sentence.

E   E   E   E   E   E   E

El   Ei   Ec   Ed   En   Ev

El Paso   Ecuador   England

O   O   O   O   O   O   O

Oahu   Olympia   Orlando

Ohio   Omaha   Ozark

DID YOU KNOW?

Ohio has a state drink.

JOINING ALERT

E is joined to the letter that follows.

O is not joined to the letter that follows.

En not *En*

The undercurve ending swings wide, then overcurves quickly into the slant stroke.

EVALUATE Circle your best joining.

29

Slant
Downcurve, loop
Downcurve,
   undercurve

Downcurve
Undercurve
Loop, curve right

MODEL THE WRITING

Model each letter and say the stroke descriptions, emphasizing the downcurve stroke in each. Ask questions such as these:
How many loops are in **E**? *(one)*
How many pauses are in **O**? *(none)*
(visual, auditory)

EVALUATE

To help students evaluate their writing, ask questions such as these:
Are your letters the correct size?
Is your **O** closed?
Is the slant of your **E** correct?
(visual, auditory)

CORRECTIVE STRATEGY

E not *E*

Slow down to form loop halfway.

PRACTICE MASTER 14

Practice Master 82 provides additional practice.

29

Curve forward,
slant
Overcurve, slant
Undercurve

Curve forward,
slant
Overcurve, slant
Overcurve, slant
Undercurve

Write Curve Forward Letters

Write the letters, joinings, and words. Then write the sentence.

n   n   n   n   n   n   n

Ni   Ne   No   Na   Ny

Nigeria   Norway   Nyack

m   m   m   m   m   m

Me   Mi   Ma   Mo   My   Mn

Mexico   Maine   Myrtle Beach

DID YOU KNOW?

Mississippi is the Magnolia State.

JOINING ALERT

n and M are joined to the letter that follows.

Me not Me

The undercurve joining must be wide to allow room for the loop in **e**.

EVALUATE Circle your best joining.

30

PRACTICE MASTER 15

Practice Master 83 provides additional practice.

MODEL THE WRITING

Model each letter and say the stroke descriptions, emphasizing the curve forward, slant strokes in each. Ask questions such as these: How does **N** differ from **M**? *(M has one more overcurve, slant.)* How many slant strokes does each letter have? *(N has two, M has three.)*
(visual, auditory)

EVALUATE

To help students evaluate their writing, ask questions such as these: Is each letter about the same width as the model? Is the second overcurve in your **M** shorter than the first? Are your slant strokes parallel?
(visual, auditory)

CORRECTIVE STRATEGY

n **not** n

Round overcurve at top.

Write the letters, joinings, and words. Then write the sentence.

K K K K K K

Ki Ke Ka Ko Kn Ky

Kiev Kansas Knoxville

H H H H H H

He Hi Ho Ha Hy

Helsinki Honolulu Hyannis

DID YOU KNOW?

Kauai is a Hawaiian island.

JOINING ALERT

K and *H* are joined to the letter that follows.

He not *He*

The loop in **H** swings across the letter and slightly down to make room for the loop in **e**.

Hawaiian Islands

Kauai

EVALUATE Circle your best joining.

31

Curve forward,
slant, (lift)
Doublecurve
Curve forward,
undercurve

Curve forward,
slant, (lift)
Curve back, slant
Retrace, loop,
curve right

MODEL THE WRITING

Model each letter and say the stroke descriptions, emphasizing the curve forward, slant strokes in each. Ask questions such as these:
How are **K** and **H** alike? *(They have the same beginning strokes and one lift.)*
How many loops are in **H**? *(one)*
(visual, auditory)

EVALUATE

To help students evaluate their writing, ask questions such as these:
Do your letters rest on the baseline?
Are your strokes smooth and even?
(visual, auditory)

CORRECTIVE STRATEGY

K **not** *K*

Touch the doublecurve to the slant stroke, then curve forward.

PRACTICE MASTER 16

Practice Master 84 provides additional practice.

31

On the chalkboard write the downcurve letters **A, C, E,** and **O** and the curve forward letters **N, M, K,** and **H.** Then have students write each letter twice. Ask these questions:

Which letters are joined to the letter that follows?

Which letter is not joined to the letter that follows?

Have students pay attention to upper-case letter formation and joinings as they write the names of

- a continent beginning with **A**
- a city beginning with **C**
- a boy beginning with **E**
- a state beginning with **O**
- a planet beginning with **N**
- a country beginning with **M**
- a girl beginning with **K**
- a family beginning with **H**

(visual, auditory, kinesthetic)

COACHING HINT

Holding the pencil too tightly is a common problem that causes students to tire easily when writing. To help students overcome this problem, have them crumple a piece of paper, place it in the palm of the writing hand, and pick up the pencil. This will serve as a reminder not to squeeze the pencil. (kinesthetic)

WRITE AWAY

Have students choose one of the events listed on page 32, imagine what it might be like, and write a paragraph describing it. Participate by sharing your ideas.

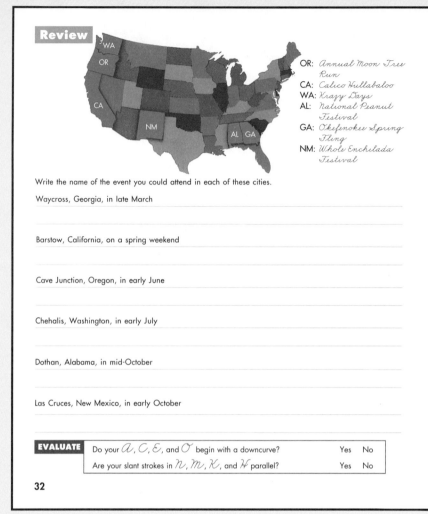

Review

OR: *Annual Moon Tree Run*
CA: *Calico Hullabaloo*
WA: *Krazy Days*
AL: *National Peanut Festival*
GA: *Okefenokee Spring Fling*
NM: *Whole Enchilada Festival*

Write the name of the event you could attend in each of these cities.

Waycross, Georgia, in late March

Barstow, California, on a spring weekend

Cave Junction, Oregon, in early June

Chehalis, Washington, in early July

Dothan, Alabama, in mid-October

Las Cruces, New Mexico, in early October

EVALUATE		
Do your *a, C, E,* and *O* begin with a downcurve?	Yes	No
Are your slant strokes in *n, m, k,* and *H* parallel?	Yes	No

32

EVALUATE

Guide students through the self-evaluation process, focusing on letter formation and slant. Encourage students to explain why one letter they wrote might be better than another. (visual, auditory)

Manuscript Maintenance

1 A	2 B	3 C	4 D	5 E	6 F	7 G	8 H	9 I	10 J	11 K	12 L	13 M
14 N	15 O	16 P	17 Q	18 R	19 S	20 T	21 U	22 V	23 W	24 X	25 Y	26 Z

Decode each riddle and its answer. Write in uppercase manuscript.

W H A T   D O E S
23 8 1 20   4 15 5 19

D E L A W A R E ?
4 5 12 1 23 1 18 5

A   N E W   J E R S E Y
1   14 5 23   10 5 18 19 5 25

W H E R E   H A S
23 8 5 18 5   8 1 19

O R E G O N ?
15 18 5 7 15 14

T O   O K L A H O M A
20 15   15 11 12 1 8 15 13 1

On Your Own Write a riddle and answer about another state.

_____

_____

_____

EVALUATE Are your letters vertical?   Yes No

33

EVALUATE

Have students focus on verticality to determine whether their uppercase manuscript letters are legible. Discuss ways to improve legibility. (visual, auditory)

MAINTAINING MANUSCRIPT

You may wish to have students do the following activities for reinforcement of manuscript writing.

1. Write their spelling words in manuscript.
2. Prepare a chart or poster in manuscript.
3. Do a crossword puzzle in manuscript.
4. Do a map in manuscript.
5. Write an outline in manuscript.

BEFORE WRITING

Discuss codes with students. Point out that secret codes have existed since earliest times. Tell them the simplest codes involve transposing letters (LHPE for HELP) or substituting other letters, numerals, or symbols for the letters of the alphabet.

MANUSCRIPT MAINTENANCE

Review the keys to legibility for manuscript writing: size and shape, slant, and spacing. Encourage students to follow these suggestions.

• Position the paper correctly.

• Pull the downstrokes in the proper direction.

• Shift the paper as your writing fills the space.

Right-handed students should pull downstrokes toward the midsection. Left-handed students should pull downstrokes toward the left elbow. Guide students in evaluating vertical quality. (visual, auditory, kinesthetic)

COACHING HINT

Practicing pull down straight strokes at the chalkboard is a good way to improve poor strokes. Place sets of two dots about six inches apart to mark the starting and stopping points of each vertical stroke. (visual, kinesthetic)

WRITE AWAY

Challenge students working in pairs to devise their own code and write a riddle and its answer. Have them use pictograms, numerals, letters, or other symbols.

Curve forward,
slant
Undercurve
Slant, undercurve

Curve forward,
slant
Undercurve
Slant
Loop back,
overcurve

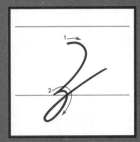

Curve forward,
slant
Overcurve,
curve down
Loop, overcurve

Write Curve Forward Letters

Write the letters, joinings, and words.

𝒰 𝒰 𝒰 𝒰 𝒰 𝒰

𝒰𝓉 𝒰𝓀 𝒰𝑔 𝒰𝒹 𝒰𝓃 𝒰𝓂

𝒰𝓉𝒶𝒽   𝒰𝑔𝒶𝓃𝒹𝒶   𝒰𝓃𝒾𝑜𝓃 𝒞𝒾𝓉𝓎

𝒴 𝒴 𝒴 𝒴 𝒴 𝒴

𝒴𝓊 𝒴𝑒 𝒴𝒶 𝒴𝑜 𝒴𝓋

𝒴𝓊𝓂𝒶   𝒴𝒶𝓀𝒾𝓂𝒶   𝒴𝑜𝓃𝓀𝑒𝓇𝓈

𝒵 𝒵 𝒵 𝒵 𝒵 𝒵

𝒵𝓊 𝒵𝑒 𝒵𝒶 𝒵𝑜

𝒵𝓊𝓇𝒾𝒸𝒽   𝒵𝒶𝓃𝑒𝓈𝓋𝒾𝓁𝓁𝑒   𝒵𝑜𝓂𝒷𝒶

JOINING ALERT

𝒰, 𝒴, and 𝒵 are joined to the letter that follows.

𝒴𝒶 not 𝒴𝓊

The overcurve ending crosses at the baseline, then continues up and wide to form the downcurve letter.

EVALUATE Circle your best joining.

34

PRACTICE MASTER 17

Practice Masters 85 and 86 provide additional practice.

MODEL THE WRITING

Model each letter and say the stroke descriptions, emphasizing the curve forward, slant strokes in each. Ask questions such as these:
How do all the letters begin? *(with a curve forward, slant)*
Which letters end with an overcurve? *(Y, Z)*
(visual, auditory)

EVALUATE

To help students evaluate their writing, ask questions such as these:
Did you pull the slant strokes in **U** to the baseline?
Do the loops of your **Y** and **Z** close at the baseline?
Is each letter about the same width as the model?
(visual, auditory)

CORRECTIVE STRATEGY

𝒴 **not** 𝒴

Pause after the undercurve.

Write the letters and words. Then write the sentence.

𝒱 𝒱 𝒱 𝒱 𝒱 𝒱

Vermont   Virginia   Vallejo

𝒳 𝒳 𝒳 𝒳 𝒳 𝒳

Xenia   Xiamen   Xuanhua

𝒲 𝒲 𝒲 𝒲 𝒲 𝒲

Wisconsin   Washington   Wyoming

DID YOU KNOW?

Xenia is a city in Ohio.

JOINING ALERT

𝒱 and 𝒲 are not joined to the letter that follows.

Joining 𝒳 is optional.

Xe   Xe

Unjoined   **Joined**

EVALUATE Circle your best word.

35

Curve forward, slant
Undercurve
Overcurve

Curve forward, slant, under-curve, (lift) Slant

Curve forward, slant
Undercurve, slant
Undercurve
Overcurve

MODEL THE WRITING

Model each letter and say the stroke descriptions, emphasizing the curve forward, slant strokes in each. Ask questions such as these:

How many undercurves are in **W**? *(two)*

How are **V** and **W** alike? *(They begin with curve forward, slant, undercurve; they end with an overcurve.)*

Where is the lift in **X**? *(after the undercurve)*

(visual, auditory)

EVALUATE

To help students evaluate their writing, ask questions such as these:

Do your letters rest on the baseline?

Are your strokes smooth and even?

(visual, auditory)

CORRECTIVE STRATEGY

𝒱   not   𝒱

Do not pause after the slant stroke; flow smoothly into the undercurve.

PRACTICE MASTER 18

Practice Masters 86 and 87 provide additional practice.

35

Slant, curve forward
and right, (lift)
Doublecurve,
curve up
Retrace, curve right

Slant, curve forward
and right, (lift)
Doublecurve,
curve up
Retrace, curve
right, (lift)
Slide right

Write Doublecurve Letters

Write the letters and words. Then write the sentence.

T T T T T T

Texas   Tom Thumb   Tyler

Tippecanoe and Tyler, too!

F F F F F F

Florida   Fort Frederica

F. Scott Fitzgerald   Fillmore

DID YOU KNOW?

Texas chose the first state tree.

JOINING ALERT

Joining *T* and *F* is optional.

Ty Fa   Ty Fa
Unjoined   **Joined**

EVALUATE Circle your best word.

36

PRACTICE MASTER 19

Name _____

Joining *T* and *F* is optional.

Write the letters and words. Then write the sentence.

T T T T T T

Ticonderoga   Tours

Transylvania   Twain

F F F F F F

Frankfurt   Fulton   France

Fort Knox   Fort Worth

"Old Folks at Home"

DID YOU KNOW?

Ticonderoga was a fort.

EVALUATE Circle your best word.

Copyright © Zaner-Bloser, Inc.   **PRACTICE MASTER 19**

Practice Master 88 provides additional practice.

36

MODEL THE WRITING

Model each letter and say the stroke descriptions, emphasizing the doublecurve in each. Ask questions such as these:
How do the letters begin? *(with a slant, curve forward and right)*
How are **T** and **F** alike? *(There is a T in F.)*
How are they different? *(In F, the last stroke is a slide right.)*
(visual, auditory)

EVALUATE

To help students evaluate their writing, ask questions such as these:
Does the last stroke in your **T** curve right?
Does your **F** have a slide right stroke?
(visual, auditory)

CORRECTIVE STRATEGY

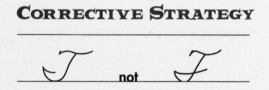

Leave space between the curve right and doublecurve strokes.

Write Overcurve Letters

Write the letters, joinings, and words.

I I I I I I I

Iowa Independence Idaho

Q Q Q Q Q Q

Queensland Quad Cities

J J J J J J J

Ju Je Ja Jo

Juneau Jamaica Joplin

JOINING ALERT

J is joined to the letter that follows.

Q is not joined to the letter that follows.

Joining *I* is optional.

In   *In*

Unjoined   **Joined**

EVALUATE Circle your best joining.

37

Overcurve
Curve down
and up
Retrace, curve
right

Curve back,
overcurve
Curve down,
retrace
Curve forward,
curve under

Overcurve
Slant
Loop back,
overcurve

MODEL THE WRITING

Model each letter and say the stroke descriptions, emphasizing the overcurve in each. Ask questions such as these:
How does **Q** begin? *(with curve back, overcurve)*
Where do **I** and **J** begin? *(just below the baseline)*
How does **J** end? *(with an overcurve)*
(visual, auditory)

EVALUATE

To help students evaluate their writing, ask questions such as these:
Do the loops of your **J** close at the baseline?
Does your **Q** end below the baseline?
Is the slant of your **I** correct?
(visual, auditory)

CORRECTIVE STRATEGY

I **not** *Q*

Make the loop an oval rather than a circle.

PRACTICE MASTER 20

Practice Masters 89 and 90 provide additional practice.

37

REFOCUS

Refer students to the cursive alphabet on page 7. Ask them to locate these six uppercase letters that begin with curve forward, slant strokes: **U, Y, Z, V, X, W**. Repeat for doublecurve letters **T** and **F** and overcurve letters **I, Q,** and **J**.

Ask these questions:

Which letters are joined to the letter that follows?

Which letters are not joined to the letter that follows?

Ask volunteers to write the letters on the chalkboard, and have students suggest words that begin with the letters. Write each word, saying the stroke descriptions for the initial uppercase letter. Highlight the stroke that names each letter grouping. (visual, auditory, kinesthetic)

COACHING HINT

Give each student a card on which one of the basic strokes is written. Tell students to write that basic stroke and then to write all the uppercase and lowercase letters that have that stroke. If time permits, have students trade cards and do the same with a different basic stroke. (visual, kinesthetic)

WRITE AWAY

Ask students to write a list of onomatopoeic words to describe sounds at the ballet, symphony, or opera. Provide examples, such as the boom of a kettledrum, the plink of a piano, or the murmur of the audience.

Review

Fort Wayne Philharmonic
Orchestra of Santa Fe
Orchestre Symphonique de Quebec
Rhode Island Philharmonic
Youngstown Symphony

Opera San Jose
Utah Symphony
Tulsa Ballet Theatre
Virginia Opera

Write where you can go to the symphony, opera, or ballet in each of these cities.

San Jose, California

Fort Wayne, Indiana

Santa Fe, New Mexico

Youngstown, Ohio

Tulsa, Oklahoma

Providence, Rhode Island

Salt Lake City, Utah

Norfolk, Virginia

Quebec, Canada

EVALUATE

| Are your uppercase letters formed correctly? | Yes | No |
| Do your letters rest on the baseline? | Yes | No |

EVALUATE

Guide students through the self-evaluation process, focusing on letter formation and slant. Encourage students to explain why one letter they wrote might be better than another. (visual, auditory)

Writing Legibly

1. Study these tips for legible writing. They will help you avoid common handwriting errors when you write.

✓ Keep loops open in letters with loops. Write *ℓ*, not *ℓ*.

✓ Close letters that should be closed. Write *a*, not *a*.

✓ Intersect strokes carefully. Write *T*, not *T*.

✓ Make sure all uppercase letters are tall. Write *M*, not *m*.

2. Look at a section from this student's social studies paper. Underline letters that need improvement.

> Are you curious about faraway
> galaxies? In 1803, Thomas Jefferson
> was curious about the unexplored
> West. He asked Meriwether Lewis
> and William Clark to go and learn
> all they could about the land
> between the mississippi River and
> the Pacific Ocean.

3. Rewrite the student's paper correctly, or write a section from one of your own papers. Pay attention to the tips for legible writing.

EVALUATE			
Did you keep loops open?		Yes	No
Did you close letters that should be closed?		Yes	No
Do your strokes intersect correctly?		Yes	No
Are all your uppercase letters tall?		Yes	No

39

Discuss the importance of legible writing in all areas of the school curriculum. Talk about how legibility affects a reader's perception of a piece of writing.

COACHING HINT

Encourage students to look through their writing folders or other school papers and select a sample that best showcases their ability to write legibly. Students may change their selections as their handwriting skills improve. (visual, kinesthetic)

EVALUATE

Guide students through the evaluation process, focusing on the featured tips for legible writing. You may wish to add to a list of tips to be displayed permanently in your classroom. (visual, auditory)

Undercurve, loop, curve forward
Doublecurve, curve up
Retrace, curve right

Undercurve, loop
Curve down and up
Retrace, curve right

Write Letters With Loops

Write the letters and words. Then write the sentence.

G *G* *G* *G* *G* *G* *G*

Georgia   Guam   Galveston

George Gershwin   Gahanna

S *S* *S* *S* *S* *S*

Salem   South Dakota   Sydney

Secretary of State Shultz

DID YOU KNOW?

Georgia has a state atlas.

JOINING ALERT

Joining *G* and *S* is optional.

Go Sa   Go Sa
Unjoined   Joined

EVALUATE Circle your best word.

40

Name

Joining *G* and *S* is optional.

Write the letters and words. Then write the sentences.

G *G* *G* *G* *G* *G* *G*

Granada Gabon Golden Gate

Gulf of Mexico The Great Gatsby

S *S* *S* *S* *S* *S* *S*

Stockholm San Jose Sydney

Serra Seward Sarasota

DID YOU KNOW?

Granada is a city in Spain.

Sydney is a seaport.

EVALUATE Circle your best word.

Copyright © Zaner-Bloser, Inc.   **PRACTICE MASTER 21**

PRACTICE MASTER 21

Practice Masters 90 and 91 provide additional practice.

40

MODEL THE WRITING

Model each letter and say the stroke descriptions, emphasizing the loop in each. Ask questions such as these:
Where do the letters begin? *(at the baseline)*
How many undercurves are in **S**? *(one)*
(visual, auditory)

EVALUATE

To help students evaluate their writing, ask questions such as these:
Is your retrace, curve right formed correctly?
Are your letters about the same width as the model?
(visual, auditory)

CORRECTIVE STRATEGY

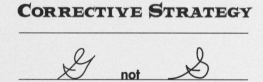

Complete curve forward; pause before doublecurve.

Write the letters and words. Then write the sentence.

L   L   L   L   L   L

Louisiana   Lynchburg   Lear

Lima   Lansing   Lend-Lease Act

D   D   D   D   D   D

Delaware   Daytona   D-Day

Dwight David Eisenhower

DID YOU KNOW?

Delaware has a state bug.

JOINING ALERT

L and *D* are not joined to the letter that follows.

Lo not *Lo*

The letter that follows begins over the ending stroke of **L**.

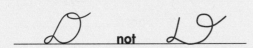

EVALUATE Circle your best word.

41

Undercurve
Loop, curve down
Loop, curve under

Doublecurve
Loop, curve down
and up
Loop, curve right

MODEL THE WRITING

Model each letter and say the stroke descriptions, emphasizing the initial loop in each. Ask questions such as these:
How many loops are in **L** and **D**? *(two)*
Where does **L** end? *(just below the baseline)*
How many times does **D** touch the baseline? *(two)*
(visual, auditory)

EVALUATE

To help students evaluate their writing, ask questions such as these:
Do all your letters have correct slant?
Does your **D** touch the baseline twice?
Does your **L** end just below the baseline?
(visual, auditory)

CORRECTIVE STRATEGY

D not *D*

Start beginning stroke farther to the right; bring ending loop to meet it.

Name

L and *D* are not joined to the letter that follows.
Write the letters and words. Then write the sentences.

L   L   L   L   L   L
Lincoln   Lod   Lyons
Lexington   Logan   Lovell

D   D   D   D   D   D
Delhi   Danbury   Degas
Defoe   Dwight David Eisenhower

DID YOU KNOW?
Lod is a city in Israel.
Delhi is a city in India.

EVALUATE Circle your best word.

PRACTICE MASTER 22   Copyright © Zaner-Bloser, Inc.

PRACTICE MASTER 22

Practice Masters 91 and 92 provide additional practice.

Undercurve, slant
Retrace, curve
forward and
back

Undercurve, slant
Retrace, curve
forward, loop
Curve forward
and back
Retrace, curve
right

Undercurve, slant
Retrace, curve
forward and
back
Curve forward,
undercurve

PRACTICE MASTER 23

Practice Masters 92 and 93 provide additional practice.

42

Write Undercurve-Slant Letters

Write the letters, joinings, and words.

P   P P P P P P

Plymouth   Point Barrow   Parr

B   B B B B B

Beloit   Benjamin Banneker

R   R R R R R R

Rh Ri Ro Ra Ry

Rhode Island   Rockford   Rye

JOINING ALERT

R is joined to the letter that follows.
P is not joined to the letter that follows.
Joining B is optional.

Ba   Ba
Unjoined   **Joined**

EVALUATE Circle your best word.

42

MODEL THE WRITING

Model each letter and say the stroke descriptions, emphasizing the undercurve-slant strokes in each. Ask questions such as these:
Which letters curve forward and back to the slant stroke? *(P, R)*
Which letter curves forward and loops? *(B)*
(visual, auditory)

EVALUATE

To help students evaluate their writing, ask questions such as these:
Do your letters have correct slant?
Is each letter about the same width as the model?
Are the forward curves of your **B** parallel with the slant stroke?
(visual, auditory)

CORRECTIVE STRATEGY

P not P

Close forward oval about halfway.

Paradise of the Pacific

Gopher State

Land of the Dakotas

Baked Bean State

Little Rhody

Write state nicknames.

On Your Own Write your state's nickname.

EVALUATE			
Do your letters have correct slant?		Yes	No
Does each *P*, *B*, and *R* begin with an undercurve?		Yes	No

43

EVALUATE

Guide students through the self-evaluation process, focusing on letter formation and slant. Encourage students to explain why one letter they wrote might be better than another. (visual, auditory)

REFOCUS

Name the letters with loops (**G, S, L, D**) and the undercurve-slant letters (**P, B, R**). Invite volunteers to write each letter on the chalkboard and answer questions such as these:

Where does your letter begin?

Where does your letter end?

Does your letter have a loop?

Does your letter join to the letter that follows?

COACHING HINT

Students who have mastered the skill of writing the uppercase and lowercase letters without models should be given writing activities that will challenge them and require thinking.

WRITE AWAY

Ask students to choose one of the states shown on page 43, make up a new nickname for it, and write a sentence explaining that nickname. Share an example with students.

KEYS TO LEGIBILITY: SIZE AND SHAPE

Discuss how both the lowercase and uppercase letters are grouped. Draw attention to the ending stroke of each letter. Model how to join a letter to

- an undercurve
- a downcurve
- an overcurve

Provide opportunities for students to practice the joinings. (visual, auditory, kinesthetic)

COACHING HINT

The joining stroke between letters must be wide enough to allow for good spacing. There should be just enough space for a minimum-sized oval. Have students practice joinings to reinforce both fluent strokes and good spacing. (visual, kinesthetic)

Practice Masters 11 and 12 provide additional practice with joinings.

Review Cursive Letters

Write each joining. Then write a word using the joining.

undercurve to undercurve	*ti*
undercurve to downcurve	*pa*
undercurve to overcurve	*in*
overcurve to undercurve	*je*
overcurve to downcurve	*zo*
overcurve to overcurve	*gy*
checkstroke to undercurve	*wh*
checkstroke to downcurve	*ba*
checkstroke to overcurve	*ov*

Write one or two sentences using some of the words you wrote above.

EVALUATE Circle your best joining.
Circle your best word.

44

EVALUATE

Guide students through the self-evaluation process, focusing on joinings. Encourage them to explain why one joining or word they wrote might be better than another. (visual, auditory)

$a, C, E, N, M, K, H, U, Y, Z, I,$ and R are joined to the letter that follows.

$O, V, W, Q, L, D,$ and P are not joined to the letter that follows.

Joining $X, T, F, I, G, S,$ and B to the letter that follows is optional.

Play Geography. Write a list of places. Each place name must begin with the last letter of the previous name. Use state and other place names. Example:

New York, Kalamazoo, Orange County

EVALUATE Circle your best word.

45

EVALUATE

Guide students through the self-evaluation process, focusing on joinings. Encourage them to explain why one joining or word they wrote might be better than another. (visual, auditory)

Certificates of Progress *should be awarded to those students who show notable handwriting progress and* Certificates of Excellence *to those who progress to the top levels of handwriting proficiency.*

Before You Go On . . .

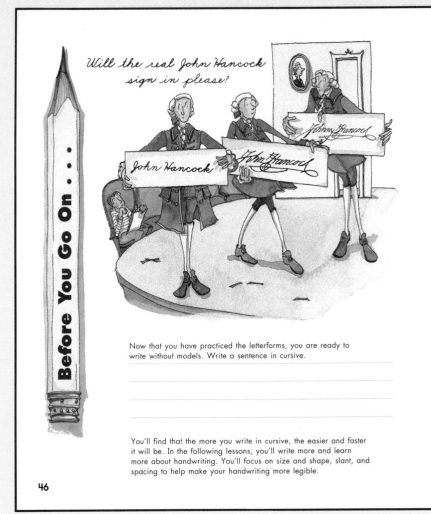

Will the real John Hancock sign in please?

John Hancock

John Hancock

John Hancock

Now that you have practiced the letterforms, you are ready to write without models. Write a sentence in cursive.

You'll find that the more you write in cursive, the easier and faster it will be. In the following lessons, you'll write more and learn more about handwriting. You'll focus on size and shape, slant, and spacing to help make your handwriting more legible.

UNIT SUMMARY

This page serves as an introduction to Unit 3. The unit is divided into three sections, each having a different handwriting emphasis: (1) size and shape, (2) slant, and (3) spacing. The lessons in each section provide opportunities for meaningful practice and application of handwriting skills in a variety of formats. Evaluations focus on the keys to legibility. The primary goal is for students to develop speed and fluency in cursive writing.

PREVIEW THE UNIT

Preview the unit with students, calling attention to these features:
• timed writing exercises
• everyday writing applications
• proofreading practice
• opportunities to use the writing process
• study of handwriting
• writing in other languages
• manuscript maintenance

Also call attention to these page features:
• writing models
• hints for writing legibly
• writing extensions
• opportunities to evaluate legibility
• facts about people, places, and things

Keys to Legibility | Size and Shape

LEGIBLE LETTERS Remember! Tall letters should not touch the headline. Short letters should be half the height of tall letters. Descenders should not go too far below the baseline.

Aa Bb Cc Dd Ee Ff Gg
Hh Ii Jj Kk Ll Mm
Nn Oo Pp Qq Rr Ss Tt
Uu Vv Ww Xx Yy Zz
1 2 3 4 5 6 7 8 9 10

Write the uppercase letters.

_____

_____

Write the tall lowercase letters.

_____

Write the short lowercase letters.

_____

Write the letters with descenders.

_____

Write the numerals 1 through 10.

_____

EVALUATE	Are all your tall letters the same size?	Yes	No
	Are all your short letters the same size?	Yes	No
	Are your numerals the same height as tall letters?	Yes	No

47

MODEL THE WRITING

Model writing a tall letter, a short letter, and a letter with a descender, noting the placement of each letter on the guidelines. Remind students that all letters of the same size should be the same height. (visual, auditory)

EVALUATE

Guide students through the self-evaluation process. Then ask if they can read their letters and numerals easily. Encourage them to explain why or why not. (visual, auditory)

BEFORE WRITING

Remind students that the word *cursive* comes from the Latin *currere*, which means "to run." Cursive was developed as a faster way to write. Poll students to find out how many can write in cursive more quickly than they can in manuscript. Tell students they will be completing a timed writing exercise to find out how quickly and legibly they can write in cursive. Ask them to keep this page in their books or writing portfolios for comparison with page 72 later in the year.

KEYS TO LEGIBILITY: SIZE AND SHAPE

Remind students that all letters of the same size should be even in height and that descenders should not go too far below the baseline. Point out that smooth handwriting is a result of *writing* letters, not drawing them. Provide opportunities to practice letters and joinings on guidelines. (visual, auditory, kinesthetic)

WRITE AWAY

Ask students to write a paragraph explaining the meaning of the sentence they wrote on page 48 and telling how it might apply to a particular experience in their lives. Participate by sharing the meaning of a favorite saying of your own.

COACHING HINT

Writing rate will increase as students begin to move the writing hand more freely. Have students practice writing letters and words in large size with crayon on folded newsprint to overcome finger motion. (kinesthetic)

Write Quickly

Practice writing quickly. Choose one of these sayings from Ben Franklin's *Poor Richard's Almanac* or a favorite saying of your own. Write the sentence as many times as you can in one minute. At the same time, try to write legibly.

Fish and visitors smell in three days.
If your head is wax, don't walk in the sun.
A small leak will sink a great ship.

LEGIBLE LETTERS   Do not draw your letters.
Write smoothly.

| EVALUATE | Can you read your writing easily? | Yes | No |
| | Can a friend read it? | Yes | No |

48

EVALUATE

Help students determine whether writing quickly has affected the size and shape of their letters. Suggest they choose a word that needs improvement and have them practice the letters and joinings in that word. (visual, auditory)

Write a Business Letter

Read this business letter. Notice its six parts.

```
                        320 North Stuart Street          ← heading
                        Winchester, Virginia 22601
                        December 5, _____

New York Public Library                                  ← inside address
5th Avenue and 42nd Street
New York, New York 10018-2788

Dear Librarian:                                          ← salutation
    I understand you have one of the world's
largest autograph collections. I will be in New York     ← body
City in March. Could you send me information
about visiting your collection?

    Thank you.

                        Sincerely,                       ← closing

                        Anina Williams                   ← signature
```

Write the body of Anina's letter or of a business letter of your own.
Pay attention to the size and shape of your letters.

_____

_____

_____

_____

_____

_____

EVALUATE   Are your short letters half the height of your tall letters?   Yes   No

49

BEFORE WRITING

Talk about philography—the hobby of collecting autographs. Ask what kinds of autographs students collect or would like to collect. Point out that some autographs are valuable. For example, in 1986 someone paid $360,000 for a letter with Thomas Jefferson's signature.

WRITE AWAY

Suggest students write a letter requesting an autograph of a favorite author, politician, actor, or sports hero. Help students locate the address of the celebrity. Remind them to use business letter form. Ask students to bring to class an envelope to be addressed after they have completed page 50.

Practice Masters 58–65 provide practice in writing across the curriculum.

EVALUATE

After students have evaluated the size of their letters, ask if their writing is legible. Ask them to explain why or why not. (visual, auditory)

49

BEFORE WRITING

Share with students several business envelopes from banks, utility companies, publishing houses, and so on. If possible, also show students envelopes addressed using calligraphy. Discuss the importance of addressing envelopes legibly.

KEYS TO LEGIBILITY: SIZE AND SHAPE

Provide opportunities for students to practice cursive numerals and punctuation marks on guidelines. (visual, auditory, kinesthetic)

WRITE AWAY

Have students address envelopes for the letters they wrote on page 49. Before stamping and mailing the envelopes, have students work in pairs to evaluate legibility.

Address an Envelope

When you address an envelope, include a return address as well as a mailing address.

Anina Williams
320 North Stuart Street
Winchester, Virginia 22601 ← **return address**

New York Public Library
5th Avenue and 42nd Street
New York, New York 10018-2788 ← **mailing address**

Address the envelope. Use the return and mailing addresses above or two addresses of your own. Adjust the size of your writing to fit the writing space.

LEGIBLE LETTERS

Remember! Numerals are the same height as tall letters.

EVALUATE Ask a friend to read and evaluate your writing. Are the addresses legible?   Yes   No

50

EVALUATE

Pair students and have them discuss the legibility of their envelopes. Encourage students to make suggestions for improving legibility. (visual, auditory)

Write Punctuation Marks

Use these punctuation marks to help clarify your writing.

- period
- comma

? question mark
' apostrophe

/ exclamation point
" " quotation marks

Write each sentence in cursive. Remember to slant punctuation marks.

"I'm thirsty," Sarah whined.

"She's bothering me!" Sam complained.

"Settle down back there!" Dad ordered.

"Are we there yet?" I asked.

On Your Own Write a sentence with at least three punctuation marks.

EVALUATE Are your question mark and exclamation points the correct size? Yes No

EVALUATE

After students have evaluated their punctuation marks, ask if their writing is legible. Ask them to explain why or why not. (visual, auditory)

BEFORE WRITING

Discuss with students how punctuation marks help clarify meaning. Write the following sentence on the chalkboard: *Judy said Ralph let's go.* Have a volunteer punctuate the sentence so that Judy is speaking to Ralph. Then ask a second student to write the sentence, punctuating it so that Ralph is speaking to Judy.

WRITE AWAY

Ask students to write the same sentence twice, punctuating it a different way each time to show a different meaning. Have volunteers write their sentences on the chalkboard without punctuation marks. Classmates can add punctuation marks to show meaning.

COACHING HINT

Correct body position influences smoothness. Encourage students to sit comfortably erect, with their feet flat on the floor and their hips touching the back of the chair. Both arms rest on the desk. The elbows are off the desk. (kinesthetic)

BEFORE WRITING

Discuss writing systems with students. Point out that we use the Roman alphabet, a writing system of 26 letters based on sounds. Other writing systems, such as Japanese, are based on syllables or words. With 74 letters, the Cambodian alphabet is the world's longest. With 11 letters, an alphabet from the Easter Islands is the world's shortest.

WRITE AWAY

Ask students to use an encyclopedia or other reference sources to research another alphabet and write a brief report on it. Alphabets that might interest students include Arabic, Cree, Hebrew, Chinese, and Cyrillic.

COACHING HINT

Draw writing lines on one side of 9" x 12" pieces of oak tag, and laminate one piece for each student. Students can use these as "slates" and practice their handwriting with a wipe-off marker. The reverse side can be used for letter activities. (visual, kinesthetic)

Write Roman Letters

This time line shows how the letters of the alphabet have evolved from picture writing. Because the Romans gave the alphabet its final form, the letters you write are Roman. Complete the time line by writing the Roman letter A above the date A.D. 114.

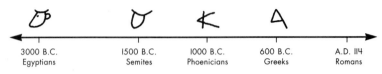

3000 B.C.	1500 B.C.	1000 B.C.	600 B.C.	A.D. 114
Egyptians	Semites	Phoenicians	Greeks	Romans

Write each Roman letter from A to Z beneath its Greek ancestor. Then break the code. Write the message below in modern Roman letters.

A	B	Γ	Δ	F	F	Γ	Θ	I	I	K	Λ	M
A	B	C	D	E	F	G	H	I	J	K	L	M

N	O	Γ	G	P	Σ	T	Υ	Υ	Υ	X	Υ	Z
N	O	P	Q	R	S	T	U	V	W	X	Y	Z

ΤΘΕ ΛΝΓΙΕΝΤ ΓΓΕΕΚΣ ΔΙΔ ΝΟΤ ΥΣΕ ΓΥΝΓΤΥΛΤΙΟΝ

THE ANCIENT GREEKS DID NOT USE PUNCTUATION

On Your Own Use the ancient Greek alphabet to write a message to a friend.

DID YOU KNOW The word *alphabet* comes from *alpha* and *beta*, the first two letters of the Greek alphabet.

52

EVALUATE

Ask students if they took more care in writing the message to a friend than in decoding the message on the page for themselves. Encourage them to explain why or why not. (visual, auditory)

Write in Spanish

What time is it?	*¿Qué hora es?*
It is 1:00.	*Es la una.*
It is 2:00.	*Son las dos.*
2:15	*dos y cuarto*
2:30	*dos y media*
2:45	*tres menos cuarto*

Write the time in Spanish. Use the word and number keys to help you.

1 una	*4 cuatro*	*7 siete*	*10 diez*
2 dos	*5 cinco*	*8 ocho*	*11 once*
3 tres	*6 seis*	*9 nueve*	*12 doce*

1. **6:00**   2. **5:15**   3. **7:45**   4. **11:15**   5. **10:30**

1. *Son las seis.*
2. Son las cinco y cuarto.
3. Son las ocho menos cuarto.
4. Son las once y cuarto.
5. Son las diez y media.

On Your Own ¿Qué hora es? Answer in Spanish to the nearest quarter hour.

EVALUATE Are all your short letters the same size?   Yes   No

53

EVALUATE

After students have evaluated the size of their letters, ask if their writing is legible. Ask them to explain why or why not. (visual, auditory)

¿Qué hora es? (keh OH rah ehs)
Es la una. (ehs lah OO nah)
Son las dos. (sohn lahs dohs)
dos y cuarto (dohs ee KWAHR toh)
dos y media (dohs ee MEH dee ah)
tres menos cuarto (trehs MEH nohs KWAHR toh)

una (OO nah)
dos (DOHS)
tres (TREHS)
cuatro (KWAH troh)
cinco (SEEN koh)
seis (SEH EES)
siete (SEE EH teh)
ocho (OH choh)
nueve (NOO EH veh)
diez (DEE ehs)
once (OHN seh)
doce (DOH seh)

BEFORE WRITING

Ask students what languages they know besides English. Discuss the advantages of knowing a second language. Invite a Spanish-speaking student to read aloud the Spanish words and expressions on the page.

KEYS TO LEGIBILITY: SIZE AND SHAPE

Invite volunteers to demonstrate the technique of drawing a horizontal line with a ruler along the tops of their letters to show proper size. (visual, kinesthetic)

WRITE AWAY

Have students choose a topic, such as meeting people or traveling by car, and compile a list of useful English words and phrases for students of English as a second language. Students who speak Spanish might write lists of Spanish words.

Practice Masters 39–57 provide additional practice in writing in Spanish.

BEFORE WRITING

Ask students if they have ever followed a dirt road or path just to see where it went. Invite students to share their experiences.

KEYS TO LEGIBILITY: SIZE AND SHAPE

Remind students to shift words with ascenders so they do not collide with descenders above them. Provide practice in writing tall letters below letters with descenders. (visual, auditory, kinesthetic)

HANDWRITING AND THE WRITING PROCESS

During prewriting, students plan for their writing by making notes, lists, and webs. "Sloppy" prewriting work may cause confusion that remains throughout the writing process, but easy-to-read notes and webs smooth the way for students, teachers, and writing partners.

As students answer the prewriting questions, discuss the possible confusion illegible writing could cause later on. Ask why legible writing might be especially important for prewriting tasks such as taking research notes or serving as a group secretary.

The Writing Process | Write About a Photograph

Prewriting

Prewriting is the thinking and planning you do before you write. Imagine that you are on this road. Jot down your thoughts to answer each question below.

Where Have You Been?

Where Are You Now?

Where Are You Going?

54

EVALUATE

Ask students to evaluate the legibility of their prewriting notes, reminding them that the notes are for their own use. Suggest that students cross out and rewrite any words they might find hard to read later. (visual, auditory, kinesthetic)

Drafting

Drafting means putting your ideas into sentences for the first time. Use your answers to the prewriting questions as you draft an entry in your travel diary about your journey. Remember to write legibly.

COLLISION
ALERT   Make sure your tall letters do not bump into the descenders above them.

_____

_____

_____

_____

_____

_____

_____

_____

_____

_____

_____

_____

_____

| **EVALUATE** | Did you avoid collisions? | Yes | No |
| | Is your writing legible? | Yes | No |

55

COACHING HINT
On the chalkboard, demonstrate the letters with descenders. Have students trace descending strokes with colored chalk to highlight their shape and size. (visual, kinesthetic)

HANDWRITING AND THE WRITING PROCESS
Students' best handwriting isn't necessary for a first draft. In fact, concentrating too much on handwriting may take students' attention away from the content of their writing. However, a "sloppy" draft makes revising and editing more difficult. As students develop a consciousness about legibility, their writing will be fluent **and** easy to read.

EVALUATE
After students have evaluated the legibility of their drafts, discuss "bumping." Ask what they did to avoid collisions. Encourage students to practice writing words with tall letters beneath words with descenders, shifting words slightly if necessary. (visual, auditory, kinesthetic)

WRITE AWAY

Have students compile a list of possible titles for their writing. Titles may correspond to the picture on page 54, such as "Dirt Road" or "In a Rut?"

HANDWRITING AND THE WRITING PROCESS

Along with spelling, punctuation, and other language mechanics, thinking about legibility should always be part of the revising and editing stages of the writing process. A checklist that includes questions related to the Keys to Legibility (size and shape, slant, and spacing) helps integrate handwriting with other language conventions and is a useful tool to incorporate into students' regular writing routine. You may wish to work as a class to devise editing symbols to use for marking spots in a draft where handwriting needs to be improved.

Publishing always requires students' best handwriting. Neat, legible writing shows courtesy to readers. It makes a good first impression, and it helps ensure that readers will understand the writer's message. Encourage students to do their personal best as they make a final copy of their work, making sure to incorporate the changes they marked during revising and editing.

  Revising and Editing

When you revise your writing, you make sure it says just what you mean. When you edit, you find and correct errors in spelling, capitalization, punctuation, and handwriting. Use the checklist below as you revise and edit your draft. You may ask a friend to read your draft and help you answer the questions.

Does your writing include all the information readers will want to know?	Yes	No
Does your writing include descriptive details?	Yes	No
Are all words spelled correctly?	Yes	No
Have you used uppercase letters and punctuation correctly?	Yes	No
Do your letters have good shape?	Yes	No
Do your letters rest on the baseline?	Yes	No
Are short letters half the height of tall letters?	Yes	No
Does your writing have uniform slant?	Yes	No
Are there good spaces between letters, words, and sentences?	Yes	No
Is your writing easy to read?	Yes	No

 Publishing

Publishing means using your best handwriting to prepare a neat, error-free copy of your work so you can share it with others. Here are some ideas for publishing your writing about a journey.

- Write several more diary entries about your journey to complete a story. Make it into an illustrated book for your school library.
- Make your writing the first entry in a travel diary you plan to keep about real and imaginary journeys.
- Share your writing with a small group of classmates. Compare the diary entries to see how different writers imagined different kinds of journeys.

56

EVALUATE

Guide students in completing the checklist and help them determine whether their writing is ready for publication. Ask why neat, legible writing is especially important for published writing. Help students select a publishing idea to pursue or announce your plans for the completion of the writing assignment. (visual, auditory, kinesthetic)

Michael Finnegan

There was an old man
named Michael Finnegan.
He had whiskers on his chinnegan.
Along came the wind and
blew them in again.
Poor old Michael Finnegan.
Begin again.

Write this American folk song in your best handwriting.
Pay special attention to the size and shape of your letters.

EVALUATE	Are your tall letters all the same size?	Yes	No
	Are your short letters half the height of your tall letters?	Yes	No
	Did you avoid collisions?	Yes	No

57

EVALUATE

As part of the self-evaluation process, have students focus on size and shape. Ask them to describe ways they might improve their writing. If necessary, have students rewrite the folk song, aiming for their personal best. (visual, auditory)

Certificates of Progress *should be awarded to those students who show notable handwriting progress and* Certificates of Excellence *to those who progress to the top levels of handwriting proficiency.*

KEYS TO LEGIBILITY: SIZE AND SHAPE

Review the cursive alphabet with students, helping them group the letters according to size.

- Tall letters should not touch the headline. Lowercase **b, d, f, h, k, l,** and **t** are tall. All uppercase letters are tall.

- Short letters are half the height of tall letters. Lowercase **a, c, e, g, i, j, m, n, o, p, q, r, s, u, v, w, x, y,** and **z** are short.

- Letters with descenders extend below the baseline. Lowercase **f, g, j, p, q, y,** and **z** have descenders. Uppercase **J, Y,** and **Z** have descenders.

Provide opportunities to practice proper placement of each letter on handwriting guidelines. (visual, auditory, kinesthetic)

WRITE AWAY

Point out that "Michael Finnegan" is a circular song. Invite students to work in small groups to write their own circular songs.

COACHING HINT

Right-handed teachers will better understand the stroke, visual perspective, and posture of the left-handed student if they practice the left-handed position themselves.

Keys to Legibility Uniform Slant

Follow these suggestions to write with uniform slant.

POSITION PULL SHIFT
Check your paper position.
Pull your downstrokes in the proper direction.
Shift your paper as you write.

If you are left-handed . . .

pull toward your left elbow.

If you are right-handed . . .

pull toward your midsection.

Write the titles of these American folk songs. Try to make your slant uniform.

"Yankee Doodle"

"Jennie Jenkins"

"John Henry"

"Mrs. Murphy's Chowder"

EVALUATE
Check your slant.
Draw lines through the slant strokes of the letters.
Your slant should look like _uniform_, not _uniform_.

58

MODEL THE WRITING

Remind students that, in cursive writing, letters slant to the right. Show an example of correct slant by writing *uniform* on guidelines. Invite a student to check the slant of your writing by drawing lines through the slant strokes of the letters. These lines should slant forward and be parallel. (visual, auditory, kinesthetic)

EVALUATE

Guide students through the self-evaluation process. Then ask if the titles students wrote are easy to read. Encourage students to explain why or why not. (visual, auditory)

When you take notes from a book, record the title and author.
Then write important or interesting information in your own words.

> *The Kids' World Almanac of the*
> *United States by T. G. Aylesworth*
> *Old laws*
> *D.C.—illegal to punch a bull*
> *in the nose*
> *Hawaii—illegal to put pennies*
> *in your ears*

Take notes on the following paragraph from *Blue Laws and True Laws* by
I.B. Sofer. As you write, pay attention to slant.

There are some unusual laws that are still on the books in the United
States. So if you're in a public eating place in New Jersey, don't slurp
your soup. If you're in Pittsburgh, don't push dirt under a rug. Don't wipe
dishes dry in Minneapolis. It's against the law!

EVALUATE | Can you read your notes easily? | Yes No
| Will you be able to read your notes next week? | Yes No

59

EVALUATE

Ask students how slant affects the legibility of their writing. Suggest
they check the slant of a word by drawing lines through the slant
strokes. Encourage them to practice pulling downstrokes in the proper
direction. (visual, auditory, kinesthetic)

BEFORE WRITING

It may interest students to know that all states have, or have had, a number of unusual laws. Among them are *blue laws*, or *Sabbath laws*. Blue laws were the first printed laws of the New Haven Colony in Connecticut. In addition to laws prohibiting business or recreation on Sunday, the following example is listed in *A General History of Connecticut*: "Every male shall have his hair cut round according to a cap."

KEYS TO LEGIBILITY: UNIFORM SLANT

Review the hints for writing with uniform slant (POSITION, PULL, SHIFT). Help students position their papers correctly and check the direction of their strokes. (visual, auditory, kinesthetic)

WRITE AWAY

Ask students to list appropriate penalties for breaking the laws listed on page 59. For example, people who sneeze in public must pay for boxes of tissues to be made available to passersby.

BEFORE WRITING

Ask how many students have visited the Smithsonian Institution in Washington, D.C. Point out that the museum houses 77 spacecraft, 12 million postage stamps, 35,594 skeletons, 30,834 costumes, 6,214 African masks, 4,500 meteorites, and many other things.

WRITE AWAY

Ask students to write a paragraph about an item they would contribute to the Smithsonian. In their paragraphs, students should explain what makes their proposed contribution valuable. Participate by suggesting an item you might contribute.

Practice Masters 58–65 provide practice in writing across the curriculum.

COACHING HINT

Holding the writing instrument correctly has an obvious effect on handwriting quality. Students having difficulty with the conventional method of holding the writing instrument may wish to try an alternate method: placing the pen or pencil between the first and second fingers. (kinesthetic)

60

Write a Paragraph

The following sentences tell about the Smithsonian Institution in Washington, D.C. Write the sentences in the correct order to make a good paragraph. Begin with the sentence that states the main idea.

Its thirteen museums are crammed with more than 100 million objects. From Teddy Roosevelt's own teddy bear to a live scorpion the size of a crab, you're bound to find something interesting to see. It's no wonder the Smithsonian is called "America's attic."

POSITION PULL SHIFT   Remember! Check the way you position your paper and the direction you pull the downstrokes.

It's no wonder the Smithsonian is called "America's attic." Its thirteen museums are crammed with more than 100 million objects. From Teddy Roosevelt's own teddy bear to a live scorpion the size of a crab, you're bound to find something interesting to see.

EVALUATE Draw lines through the slant strokes in your letters. Is your slant uniform?   Yes   No

DID YOU KNOW ? Washington, D.C., is a city without a state.

60

EVALUATE

After students have evaluated their slant, have them describe what they did to make their slant uniform. Ask if their writing is legible, and have them explain why or why not. (visual, auditory)

Edit Your Writing

Use these proofreading marks to edit your writing.

- ≡ Capitalize.
- / Use lowercase.
- ⊙ Add period.
- ∧ Insert (add).
- ⤶ Delete (take out).
- ¶ Indent for paragraph.

Write this paragraph correctly. Make the changes indicated by the proofreading marks.

¶ Ȧnyone *Your* can have a good time at a museum. Just follow *these* the Rules. Eat something *food* before you go. ẉear comfortable shoes. Don't try to see everything! Just pick *one or two* exhibits that interest you⊙

_____

_____

_____

_____

_____

_____

EVALUATE Does your writing have uniform slant?   Yes   No

EVALUATE

After students have evaluated their slant, ask if their writing is legible. Have them explain why or why not. (visual, auditory)

BEFORE WRITING

Discuss the role of editing and the use of proofreading marks in the writing process. On the chalkboard, write several sentences with various errors. Demonstrate how to use the proofreading marks to show the errors.

KEYS TO LEGIBILITY: UNIFORM SLANT

Evaluate slant by drawing lines through the slant strokes of the letters. The lines should be parallel and should show uniform forward slant. (visual, kinesthetic)

WRITE AWAY

Ask students to compile a list of additional "rules" for museum-goers. Students should include rules that will ensure they have fun at the museum, for example, "Strike a pose next to your favorite statue, and ask someone to take your picture."

BEFORE WRITING

Share with students a variety of forms, including contest entry forms, magazine subscription forms, and catalog order forms. Discuss what the forms have in common.

MANUSCRIPT MAINTENANCE

Remind students that manuscript writing is vertical. To achieve verticality, right-handed students should pull the downstrokes toward the midsection. Left-handed students should pull the downstrokes toward the left elbow. Ask students to write their names in manuscript. Guide them in evaluating vertical quality. (visual, auditory, kinesthetic)

The form on page 62 is reproduced on Practice Master 24.

WRITE AWAY

Ask students to use manuscript writing to design forms for various uses in the classroom. Students can then trade and complete forms.

COACHING HINT

Write the same word on the chalkboard in cursive and in manuscript. Use parallel lines of colored chalk to highlight the difference between manuscript verticality and cursive slant.

Manuscript Maintenance

Fill out the conference registration form below. Use the information that follows or information that you supply. Please print.

Zach Tyler
2500 Dearborn Avenue
Skokie, Illinois 60076
School: Pierce Middle School
Grade: 5
Book Title: I Can Draw
Book Description: This is a how-to book with directions for using a compass to draw geometric designs.

Young Authors' Roundtable
[ ] YES! I would like to attend the Young Authors' Roundtable
at the City Civic Center on May 25, _____.

NAME (Please print.)
_____

ADDRESS
_____

CITY   STATE   ZIP
_____

SCHOOL   GRADE
_____

What is the title of the book you have written?
_____

Write a short description of your book.
_____
_____
_____

EVALUATE   Ask a friend to read and evaluate your writing.
Is the completed application legible?   Yes   No

62

EVALUATE

Pair students and have them discuss the legibility of their application forms. Encourage students to make suggestions for improving legibility. (visual, auditory)

 ## MAINTAINING MANUSCRIPT

Students should remember that the keys to legibility apply to the manuscript maintenance activities. It is recommended that teachers review their application regularly, since students will have frequent situations that require manuscript writing. The difference in the slant (vertical quality) of manuscript is the most obvious variation, and students need to be able to make this adjustment readily. By visualizing parallel vertical lines over the pull down straight strokes of the manuscript, the student can quickly evaluate the vertical quality of the manuscript writing.

Write Your Signature

As president of the Continental Congress in 1776, John Hancock signed the Declaration of Independence with a flourish. Circle the bold signature for which Hancock became famous.

Experiment with your signature. Write your initials, your nickname, your full name, and any other form of your name that you like. Write in manuscript and cursive, with large letters and small letters.

Write your name as if you were signing the Declaration of Independence.

 Circle the signature that shows the real you.

DID YOU KNOW *Put your John Hancock here* means "Write your signature."

EVALUATE

Ask students if their signatures are legible. Ask them to explain why or why not. (visual, auditory)

BEFORE WRITING

Write your signature on the chalkboard. Point out that a person's signature is an important and personal part of writing. Since no two people are alike, each person's signature is unique. Discuss how personality can affect the way a person signs his or her name.

WRITE AWAY

Ask students to write a paragraph analyzing their signatures. In their paragraphs, students should tell what they think their signatures reveal about them.

COACHING HINT

Correct paper placement is a factor in legibility. Remind students to check this periodically. (kinesthetic)

BEFORE WRITING

Share the following information with students: "Spoonbridge and Cherry," designed by Claes Oldenburg and Coosje van Bruggen, is 52 feet long and 29 feet high. The sculpture is a working fountain. Water flows from both the base of the cherry and the top of the stem.

KEYS TO LEGIBILITY: UNIFORM SLANT

Most errors in slant can be corrected in one of the following ways:

1. Check paper position.

2. Pull the downstrokes in the proper direction.

3. Shift the paper as the writing progresses across the line. (visual, kinesthetic)

HANDWRITING AND THE WRITING PROCESS

During prewriting, students plan for their writing by making notes, lists, and webs. "Sloppy" prewriting work may cause confusion that remains throughout the writing process, but easy-to-read notes and webs smooth the way for students, teachers, and writing partners.

As students make prewriting lists, discuss the possible confusion illegible writing could cause later on. Ask why legible writing might be especially important for prewriting tasks such as taking research notes or serving as a group secretary.

The Writing Process | Write About a Sculpture

Prewriting

Prewriting helps you collect your ideas before you write. This sculpture in the Minneapolis Sculpture Garden is called "Spoonbridge and Cherry." Look at it carefully. In the columns below, write the details you notice.

Spoonbridge and Cherry, 1985-1988 Aluminum, Stainless Steel, Paint (354 x 618 x 162")
by C. Oldenburg and C. van Bruggen
Collection Walker Art Center, Minneapolis.
Gift of Frederick R. Weisman in honor of his parents, William and Mary Weisman.
1988

What Do You See?   **Where Do You See It?**

64

EVALUATE

Ask students to evaluate the legibility of their prewriting lists, reminding them that the lists are for their own use. Suggest that students cross out and rewrite any words they might find hard to read later. (visual, auditory, kinesthetic)

Drafting

When you draft, you put your ideas into sentences for the first time. Use the details you listed as you draft a paragraph that describes the sculpture for someone who has not seen it. Help your reader form a mental picture. Remember to write legibly.

LEGIBLE LETTERS

Slant strokes in letters should be parallel.

EVALUATE	Ask a friend to read and evaluate your writing.		
	Is the slant uniform?	Yes	No
	Is the paragraph legible?	Yes	No

COACHING HINT

To help students improve slant, draw parallel slant lines and have a student change them into the slant strokes of a word. (visual, kinesthetic)

HANDWRITING AND THE WRITING PROCESS

Students' best handwriting isn't necessary for a first draft. In fact, concentrating too much on handwriting may take students' attention away from the content of their writing. However, a "sloppy" draft makes revising and editing more difficult. As students develop a consciousness about legibility, their writing will be fluent **and** easy to read.

EVALUATE

Pair students and have them discuss how slant affects the legibility of their writing. Suggest students look at the slant of one group of letters in their words (for example, undercurve letters) and check if the slant is uniform. Encourage students to write several rows of any troublesome letters, using the hints for writing with uniform slant. (visual, auditory, kinesthetic)

WRITE AWAY

Ask students to write a paragraph about an imaginary sculpture. Then have pairs of students exchange paragraphs and draw their partner's sculpture based on the description.

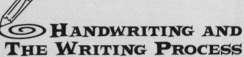

HANDWRITING AND THE WRITING PROCESS

Along with spelling, punctuation, and other language mechanics, thinking about legibility should always be part of the revising and editing stages of the writing process. A checklist that includes questions related to the Keys to Legibility (size and shape, slant, and spacing) helps integrate handwriting with other language conventions and is a useful tool to incorporate into students' regular writing routine. You may wish to work as a class to devise editing symbols to use for marking spots in a draft where handwriting needs to be improved.

Publishing always requires students' best handwriting. Neat, legible writing shows courtesy to readers. It makes a good first impression, and it helps ensure that readers will understand the writer's message. Encourage students to do their personal best as they make a final copy of their work, making sure to incorporate the changes they marked during revising and editing.

 Revising and Editing

Revising means making sure your writing says just what you mean. Editing involves finding and correcting errors in spelling, capitalization, punctuation, and handwriting. Use the checklist below as you revise and edit your draft. You may ask a friend to read your draft and help you answer the questions.

Does your writing include all the information readers will want to know?	Yes	No
Does your writing include descriptive details?	Yes	No
Are all words spelled correctly?	Yes	No
Have you used uppercase letters and punctuation correctly?	Yes	No
Do your letters have good size and shape?	Yes	No
Does your writing have uniform slant?	Yes	No
Do all the slant strokes in your letters slant the same way?	Yes	No
Are there good spaces between letters, words, and sentences?	Yes	No
Is your writing easy to read?	Yes	No

 Publishing

Publishing means using your best handwriting to prepare a neat, error-free copy of your work so you can share it with others. Here are some ideas for publishing your writing about a sculpture.

- Work as a class to write descriptions of other landmarks in the United States. Include your writing along with maps and illustrations in a book to share with other classes.
- Make a travel brochure that includes your writing and a picture you draw. Give the brochure to your local library.
- Share your writing with a small group of classmates. Compare the details each writer noticed and the descriptive words each writer used.

66

EVALUATE

Guide students in completing the checklist and help them determine whether their writing is ready for publication. Ask why neat, legible writing is especially important for published writing. Help students select a publishing idea to pursue or announce your plans for the completion of the writing assignment. (visual, auditory, kinesthetic)

Evaluate Slant

Oh, Susannah

I came from Salem City
with my washpan on my knee.
I'm going to California.
The gold dust for to see.
It rained all night the day I left,
The weather it was dry.
The sun so hot I froze to death,
Oh, brothers, don't you cry!

Write these lines from an American folk song in your best handwriting.
Pay special attention to slant.

_____

_____

_____

_____

_____

_____

_____

_____

_____

_____

EVALUATE | Does your writing have uniform slant?   Yes   No

67

KEYS TO LEGIBILITY: UNIFORM SLANT

Remind students that in cursive writing all letters slant to the right. Review the hints for writing with uniform slant for both left-handed and right-handed writers.

• Position your paper correctly.

• Pull the downstrokes in the proper direction.

• Shift your paper to the left as you write.

Invite both left-handed and right-handed students to model for class-mates. (visual, auditory, kinesthetic)

WRITE AWAY

Ask students to revise the first stanza of "Oh, Susannah" to tell a modern-day story about someone moving from one part of the country to another. Participate by sharing an opening line, such as "I came from Texarkana, a computer in my bag."

EVALUATE

Guide students through the self-evaluation process, focusing on slant. Ask students whether improvement is needed. If necessary, have students rewrite the folk song, aiming for their personal best. (visual, auditory)

Certificates of Progress *should be awarded to those students who show notable handwriting progress and Certificates of Excellence to those who progress to the top levels of handwriting proficiency.*

Keys to Legibility | Correct Spacing

These sentences are legible. The spacing is correct.

Between Letters There should be space for *o*.
Between Words There should be space for \.
Between Sentences There should be space for *O*

to see. O It rained

Write these lines from the song "Oh, Susannah" in paragraph form.
For correct spacing, shift your paper as you write.

I soon shall be in Frisco and there I'll look around. And when I see the gold lumps there, I'll pick them off the ground.

EVALUATE

Is there space for *o* between letters?	Yes	No
Is there space for \ between words?	Yes	No
Is there space for *O* between sentences?	Yes	No

68

MODEL THE WRITING

To show an example of correct spacing, write the following sentences on guidelines: *Don't you cry for me. I'm going to California.* Invite volunteers to check the spacing by drawing ovals between letters, by drawing slanted lines between words, and by writing uppercase **O** between sentences. (visual, auditory, kinesthetic)

EVALUATE

Guide students through the self-evaluation process. Then ask if their sentences are easy to read. Encourage students to explain why or why not. (visual, auditory)

Write Lead Sentences

A lead sentence is the first sentence of a story. It may tell *who*, *what*, *when*, and *where*. Sometimes it tells *why*.

James Wilson Marshall *discovered gold*
who   what

at Sutter's Mill *this morning*
where   when

Use the facts to write lead sentences.

Who: *Mrs. O'Leary's cow*   Where: *in the O'Leary barn*
What: *kicked over a lantern*   When: *last night*

_____

_____

Who: *Abolitionist Sojourner Truth*
What: *spoke*   When: *yesterday*
Where: *at Seneca Falls*   Why: *to get voting rights*

_____

_____

On Your Own Write a lead sentence about either a school event or a historical event. Try to include the five W's: *who*, *what*, *when*, *where*, and *why*.

_____

_____

EVALUATE Is there space for *O* between letters?   Yes   No

69

BEFORE WRITING

Share with students lead sentences of articles in a newspaper. Discuss which of the five *W*'s (*who, what, when, where,* and *why*) are covered by the story leads.

KEYS TO LEGIBILITY: CORRECT SPACING

Remind students that shifting their papers as they write can help keep spacing consistent. (visual, kinesthetic)

WRITE AWAY

Ask students to complete the story they began on page 69. Point out that in the process of writing, students may want to revise their story leads.

EVALUATE

After students have evaluated the spacing between their letters, ask if their writing is legible. Have them explain why or why not. (visual, auditory)

BEFORE WRITING

On the chalkboard write these two simple sentences:

Did Benjamin Franklin win the debate?
Did the bald eagle become our national bird?

Demonstrate how to use a comma and the word *or* to combine the sentences.

KEYS TO LEGIBILITY: CORRECT SPACING

Remind students that a little more space is needed before words that begin with a downcurve letter (**a, c, d, q, g, o**). (visual, auditory)

WRITE AWAY

Ask students if they are pleased with the selection of the bald eagle as our national bird. Ask them to write a paragraph in support of the eagle or another bird. Suggest students write a statement of opinion followed by supporting facts.

70

Write Compound Sentences

Two simple sentences can be combined to form a compound sentence.

Is the bald eagle graceful and powerful, or is it mean and cowardly?

Use a comma and the word in parentheses to combine each pair of sentences.

Ben Franklin wanted the turkey to represent our country.
Congress chose the bald eagle. (but)

Franklin praised the turkey's courage.
He condemned the bald eagle's cowardice. (and)

Is the turkey bold and fierce?
Is it vain and silly? (or)

EVALUATE Is there space for \ between words?   Yes   No

70

EVALUATE

After students have evaluated the spacing between their words, ask if their writing is legible. Have them explain why or why not. (visual, auditory)

Manuscript Maintenance

Use an encyclopedia to complete the chart about the North Central States.
Write in manuscript.

LEGIBLE LETTERS Write smaller to fit the writing space.

The North Central States

State	Capital	State Song
North Dakota	Bismark	"North Dakota Hymn"
South Dakota	Pierre	"Hail! South Dakota"
Nebraska	Lincoln	"Beautiful Nebraska"
Kansas	Topeka	"Home on the Range"
Minnesota	St. Paul	"Hail! Minnesota"
Iowa	Des Moines	"The Song of Iowa"
Missouri	Jefferson City	"Missouri Waltz"
Wisconsin	Madison	"On, Wisconsin"
Illinois	Springfield	"Illinois"
Michigan	Lansing	"My Michigan"
Ohio	Columbus	"Beautiful Ohio"
Indiana	Indianapolis	"On the Banks of the Wabash, Far Away"

EVALUATE Did you adjust your writing to fit the space? Yes No
Is the chart legible? Yes No

DID YOU KNOW? "The Star-Spangled Banner" is our national anthem.

EVALUATE

Have students focus on spacing to determine whether their charts
are legible. Discuss how students can improve their spacing. (visual,
auditory)

MAINTAINING MANUSCRIPT

To emphasize the need for manuscript, discuss situations that require
manuscript writing. If possible, provide samples of job applications,
subscription cards, test forms, tax returns, and bank forms as examples of the need for manuscript writing. Allow students to practice
filling out a form requiring name, address, age, and phone number.
Discuss potential problems with these forms if the manuscript is illegible, and role-play such situations.

BEFORE WRITING

On a map of the United States, locate
the North Central States. Ask a volunteer to identify the lakes for which the
region is known (four of the Great
Lakes: Huron, Michigan, Erie, and
Superior).

MANUSCRIPT MAINTENANCE

Review the keys to legibility for manuscript writing: size and shape, slant,
and spacing. Show an example of correct spacing between letters, words,
and sentences. Remind students that letters and words too close together or too
far apart make writing difficult to read.
Provide opportunities for them to practice good spacing. (visual, auditory,
kinesthetic)

WRITE AWAY

Ask students to compile a list of interesting facts about the North Central States,
for example, Minnesota is the home of
the oldest rock. Students can use an
almanac or an encyclopedia as a
source of information.

COACHING HINT

Demonstrate the placement of lightly
drawn lines over manuscript letters as
a check of vertical quality. (visual, auditory, kinesthetic)

*Practice Masters 58–65 provide manuscript
writing practice.*

BEFORE WRITING

Remind students that on page 48 they completed a timed writing exercise to find out how quickly and legibly they could write. The writing exercise on this page will enable students to evaluate their progress.

KEYS TO LEGIBILITY: CORRECT SPACING

Remind students that shifting their papers as they write can help keep spacing consistent. (auditory, kinesthetic)

WRITE AWAY

Ask students to write three interesting sayings or idiomatic expressions. Suggest they use a book of proverbs or an almanac as a source of expressions. Participate by sharing these idioms: *Where six can eat, seven can eat* (Spanish); *You can't dance at two weddings at the same time* (Yiddish).

Write Quickly

Practice writing quickly. Choose one of these sayings from Ben Franklin's *Poor Richard's Almanac* or a favorite saying of your own. Write the sentence as many times as you can in one minute. At the same time, try to write legibly.

The cat in gloves catches no mice.
A lie stands on one leg, truth on two.
The honey is sweet, but the bee has a sting.

LEGIBLE LETTERS   Do not draw your letters. Write smoothly.

| EVALUATE | Can you read your writing easily? | Yes No |
| | Can a friend read it? | Yes No |

72

EVALUATE

Have students determine whether writing quickly has affected legibility. Suggest they compare this writing with their writing on page 48 to see if they are writing more quickly and legibly. (visual, auditory)

72

Write in French

What time is it?	*Quelle heure est-il?*
It is ...	*Il est ...*
1:00	*une heure*
2:00	*deux heures*
2:15	*deux heures et quart*
2:30	*deux heures et demie*
2:45	*trois heures moins le quart*

Write the time in French. Use the word and number keys to help you.

1 un	*4 quatre*	*7 sept*	*10 dix*
2 deux	*5 cinq*	*8 huit*	*11 onze*
3 trois	*6 six*	*9 neuf*	*12 douze*

1. **6:00**   2. **5:15**   3. **7:45**   4. **11:15**   5. **10:30**

1. *Il est six heures.*
2. Il est cinq heures et quart.
3. Il est huit heures moins le quart.
4. Il est onze heures et quart.
5. Il est dix heures et demie.

On Your Own Quelle heure est-il? Answer in French to the nearest quarter hour.

EVALUATE Is your spacing correct?   Yes   No

BEFORE WRITING

Review telling time in Spanish on page 53. In French, as in Spanish, there is no word for *after* or *until* when telling time. Minutes are added to or subtracted from the hour. Invite a French-speaking student to read aloud the French words and expressions on the page.

WRITE AWAY

For each time shown on page 73, ask students to write a sentence telling what they are likely to be doing. Participate by telling what you generally do at 6:00 in the morning or evening. Students who speak French might write their sentences in French.

COACHING HINT

Use the keys to legibility for frequent handwriting evaluation in all curriculum areas. Display students' handwriting examples that show excellence. (visual)

EVALUATE

After students have evaluated the spacing between their letters, ask if their writing is legible. Have them explain why or why not. (visual, auditory)

Quelle heure est-il? (kehl ur eh=teel)
Il est. . . (ee=leh)
une heure (oo=nur)
deux heures (doo=zur)
deux heures et quart (doo=zur ay kar)
deux heures et demie (doo=zur ay duh MEE)
trois heures moins le quart (trwah=zur mwan luh kar)
un (UHN)
deux (DOO)
trois (TRWAH)
quatre (KAH tr)
cinq (SANK)
six (SEES)
sept (SET)
huit (WEET)
neuf (NOOF)
dix (DEES)
onze (OHNZ)
douze (DOOZ)
Il est six heures. (ee=leh se=zur)

73

BEFORE WRITING

Discuss Thanksgiving with students. Ask what students picture in their minds when they hear the word *Thanksgiving*. Use a word web to record students' responses.

KEYS TO LEGIBILITY: CORRECT SPACING

Remind students there should be enough space for $\mathcal{O}$ between letters, \ between words, and $\mathcal{O}$ between sentences. (visual, auditory)

HANDWRITING AND THE WRITING PROCESS

During prewriting, students plan for their writing by making notes, lists, and webs. "Sloppy" prewriting work may cause confusion that remains throughout the writing process, but easy-to-read notes and webs smooth the way for students, teachers, and writing partners.

As students write their brainstorming lists, discuss the possible confusion illegible writing could cause later on. Ask why legible writing might be especially important for prewriting tasks such as taking research notes or serving as a group secretary.

The Writing Process Write About a Painting

Prewriting

Before you write to describe, it's a good idea to do prewriting by exploring your five senses. Step into Doris Lee's painting "Thanksgiving." Work alone or with a partner to brainstorm words that describe the experience. Write the words below.

What I Touch

Doris Lee's "Thanksgiving"

What I See

What I Taste

What I Smell

What I Hear

74

EVALUATE

Ask students to evaluate the legibility of their brainstorming notes, reminding them that the webs are for their own use. Suggest that students cross out and rewrite any words they might find hard to read later. (visual, auditory, kinesthetic)

Drafting

Drafting means putting your ideas into sentences for the first time. Use the words from your brainstorming list as you write a draft about spending Thanksgiving inside the painting. Write in the first person, using the pronoun *I*. Remember to write legibly.

LEGIBLE
LETTERS

Shift your paper as you write.

EVALUATE	Is your spacing correct?	Yes	No
	Is the paragraph legible?	Yes	No

DID YOU KNOW?

In 1789 George Washington proclaimed November 26 a day of national thanksgiving.

75

An occasional check for correct paper and pencil positions is important to maintain good handwriting skills and to help with legibility. (visual, auditory, kinesthetic)

HANDWRITING AND THE WRITING PROCESS

Students' best handwriting isn't necessary for a first draft. In fact, concentrating too much on handwriting may take students' attention away from the content of their writing. However, a "sloppy" draft makes revising and editing more difficult. As students develop a consciousness about legibility, their writing will be fluent **and** easy to read.

EVALUATE

After students have evaluated their writing, discuss the importance of spacing issues in written work. These might include indenting paragraphs, leaving ample margins, and hyphenating words to avoid stretching or crowding letters at the end of a line. (visual, auditory)

WRITE AWAY

Ask students to write a short description of the first Thanksgiving. Students can use an encyclopedia or other reference source for information. Participate by sharing the following facts: The first Thanksgiving meal was a breakfast. Native Americans brought turkeys, pumpkins, corn, sweet potatoes, and cranberries to the celebration. Boiled eel, lobster, roast pigeon, and stuffed cod were also served.

HANDWRITING AND THE WRITING PROCESS

Along with spelling, punctuation, and other language mechanics, thinking about legibility should always be part of the revising and editing stages of the writing process. A checklist that includes questions related to the Keys to Legibility (size and shape, slant, and spacing) helps integrate handwriting with other language conventions and is a useful tool to incorporate into students' regular writing routine. You may wish to work as a class to devise editing symbols to use for marking spots in a draft where handwriting needs to be improved.

Publishing always requires students' best handwriting. Neat, legible writing shows courtesy to readers. It makes a good first impression, and it helps ensure that readers will understand the writer's message. Encourage students to do their personal best as they make a final copy of their work, making sure to incorporate the changes they marked during revising and editing.

 Revising and Editing

You revise your writing by making sure it says just what you mean. When you edit, you find and correct errors in spelling, capitalization, punctuation, and handwriting. Use the checklist below as you revise and edit your draft. You may ask a friend to read your draft and help you answer the questions.

Does your writing include all the information readers will want to know?	Yes	No
Does your writing include descriptive details?	Yes	No
Are all words spelled correctly?	Yes	No
Have you used uppercase letters and punctuation correctly?	Yes	No
Do your letters have good size and shape?	Yes	No
Does your writing have uniform slant?	Yes	No
Is there space for ∅ between letters?	Yes	No
Is there space for \ between words?	Yes	No
Is there space for ⊙ between sentences?	Yes	No
Is your writing easy to read?	Yes	No

 Publishing

Publishing means using your best handwriting to prepare a neat, error-free copy of your work so you can share it with others. Here are some ideas for publishing your writing about a painting.

- Use your writing to make a picture book about Thanksgiving to share with younger children.
- Write to describe how you usually spend Thanksgiving. Include your two pieces of writing in a bulletin board display in your classroom.
- Read your writing aloud to a small group of classmates. Compare how different writers used details from each of the five senses.

EVALUATE

Guide students in completing the checklist and help them determine whether their writing is ready for publication. Ask why neat, legible writing is especially important for published writing. Help students select a publishing idea to pursue or announce your plans for the completion of the writing assignment. (visual, auditory, kinesthetic)

Evaluate Spacing

'Twas Midnight

'Twas midnight on the ocean,
Not a streetcar was in sight;
The sun was shining brightly,
For it rained all day that night.
'Twas a summer day in winter
And snow was raining fast.
As a barefoot boy with shoes on
Stood sitting in the grass.

Write this American folk rhyme in your best handwriting.
Pay special attention to spacing.

EVALUATE	Is there space for $\mathcal{O}$ between letters?	Yes	No
	Is there space for \ between words?	Yes	No

77

KEYS TO LEGIBILITY: CORRECT SPACING

Display an example of correct spacing between letters, words, and sentences.

Between Letters There should be enough space for $\mathcal{O}$.

Between Words There should be enough space for \.

Between Sentences There should be enough space for $\mathcal{O}$.

Provide opportunities for students to write two or more sentences and to check the spacing between letters, words, and sentences. (auditory, visual, kinesthetic)

WRITE AWAY

"'Twas Midnight" has been called an "upside-down, inside-out" poem. Ask students to write their own version of the poem by replacing key words with their opposites or near opposites. Students can begin: "'Twas noontime on the desert/Not a paddleboat was in sight."

EVALUATE

Guide students through the self-evaluation process, focusing on spacing. Ask students whether or not improvement is needed. If necessary, have them rewrite the rhyme, aiming for their personal best. (visual, auditory)

Certificates of Progress *should be awarded to those students who show notable handwriting progress and* Certificates of Excellence *to those who progress to the top levels of handwriting proficiency.*

Remind students that on page 5, as a pretest, they wrote the first stanza of this folk song and evaluated their handwriting. They will write the same stanza for the posttest. Tell them to use correct letter size and shape, uniform slant, and correct spacing as they write. (visual, auditory, kinesthetic)

Posttest

This Land Is Your Land

This land is your land, this land is my land
From California to the New York island,
From the redwood forest to the Gulf Stream waters
This land was made for you and me.

As I was walking that ribbon of highway,
I saw above me that endless skyway,
I saw below me that golden valley
This land was made for you and me.

Woody Guthrie

On your paper, write the first stanza of this American folk song in your best cursive writing.

EVALUATE	Is your writing legible? Yes No

78

EVALUATE

Have students use the keys to legibility to evaluate their handwriting. Suggest they compare this writing with their writing on the pretest. Discuss how their writing has changed. Meet individually with students to help them assess their progress. (visual, auditory)

Record of Student's Handwriting Skills

Cursive

	Needs Improvement	Shows Mastery
Sits correctly	☐	☐
Holds pencil correctly	☐	☐
Positions paper correctly	☐	☐
Writes numerals 1–10	☐	☐
Writes undercurve letters: **i, t, u, w**	☐	☐
Writes undercurve letters: **r, s, p, j**	☐	☐
Writes downcurve letters: **a, c, d, q , g, o**	☐	☐
Writes overcurve letters: **n, m, x, y, z, v**	☐	☐
Writes letters with loops: **e, l, h, k, f, b**	☐	☐
Writes downcurve letters: **A, C, E, O**	☐	☐
Writes curve forward letters: **N, M, K, H**	☐	☐
Writes curve forward letters: **U, Y, Z, V, X, W**	☐	☐
Writes doublecurve letters: **T, F**	☐	☐
Writes overcurve letters: **I, Q, J**	☐	☐
Writes letters with loops: **G, S, L, D**	☐	☐
Writes undercurve-slant letters: **P, B, R**	☐	☐
Writes the undercurve to undercurve joining	☐	☐
Writes the undercurve to downcurve joining	☐	☐
Writes the undercurve to overcurve joining	☐	☐
Writes the overcurve to undercurve joining	☐	☐
Writes the overcurve to downcurve joining	☐	☐
Writes the overcurve to overcurve joining	☐	☐
Writes the checkstroke to undercurve joining	☐	☐
Writes the checkstroke to downcurve joining	☐	☐
Writes the checkstroke to overcurve joining	☐	☐
Writes with correct size and shape	☐	☐
Writes with uniform slant	☐	☐
Writes with correct spacing	☐	☐
Writes quickly	☐	☐
Regularly checks written work for legibility	☐	☐

79

The form on page 79 is reproduced on Practice Master 25.

COACHING HINT
If a student needs improvement, reevaluate his or her writing following practice over a period of time. Invite the student to share in the evaluation. (visual, auditory)

EVALUATE
This chart provides a place for you to record the student's handwriting progress. The chart lists the essential skills in the program. After each skill has been practiced and evaluated, you can indicate whether the student *Shows Mastery* or *Needs Improvement* by checking the appropriate box.

Shows Mastery Mastery of written letterforms is achieved when the student writes the letters using correct basic strokes. Compare the student's written letterforms with the letter models. Keep in mind the keys to legibility (size and shape, slant, and spacing) when evaluating letters, numerals, punctuation marks, words, and sentences.

Needs Improvement If a student has not mastered a skill, provide additional basic instruction and practice. To improve letterforms, have the student practice writing the letter in isolation and within words and sentences. Reinforce instruction through activities geared to the student's modality strengths. When mastery of the skill is achieved, check *Shows Mastery*.

Index